Agile Project Management: Running PRINCE2™ projects with DSDM™ Atern™

London: TSO

Published by TSO (The Stationery Office) and available from:

Online
www.tsoshop.co.uk

Mail, Telephone, Fax & E-mail
TSO
PO Box 29, Norwich NR3 1GN
Telephone orders/General enquiries: 0870 600 5522
Fax orders: 0870 600 5533
E-mail: customer.services@tso.co.uk
Textphone: 0870 240 3701

TSO Shops
16 Arthur Street, Belfast BT1 4GD
028 9023 8451 Fax 028 9023 5401
71 Lothian Road, Edinburgh EH3 9AZ
0870 606 5566 Fax 0870 606 5588

TSO@Blackwell and other Accredited Agents

The information contained in this publication is believed to be correct at the time of manufacture. Whilst care has been taken to ensure that the information is accurate, the publisher can accept no responsibility for any errors or omissions or for changes to the details given.

Keith Richards has asserted his moral rights under the Copyright, Designs and Patents Act 1988 to be identified as the author of this work.

DSDM and DSDM are registered trade marks and Atern is a trade mark of Dynamic Systems Development Method Limited. DSDM and Atern graphics are copyright of Dynamic Systems Development Method Limited and reproduced by kind permission; applications to reuse, reproduce or republish should be sent to info@dsdm.org

The PRINCE2 Cityscape logo™ is a Trade Mark of the Office of Government Commerce, and is Registered in the U.S. Patent and Trademark Office

PRINCE® is a Registered Trade Mark and a Registered Community Trade Mark of the Office of Government Commerce, and is Registered in the U.S. Patent and Trademark Office

PRINCE2™ is a Trade Mark of the Office of Government Commerce

The Swirl logo™ is a Trade Mark of the Office of Government Commerce

A CIP catalogue record for this book is available from the British Library

A Library of Congress CIP catalogue record has been applied for

First published 2007

ISBN 978 0 11 331058 6

Printed in the United Kingdom by The Stationery Office, London.

N5563601 C/4 7/07

Contents

List of figures   v

List of tables   v

Acknowledgements   vi

Maturity mark   vi

PART 1 RATIONALE FOR INTEGRATION   1

1   Introduction   3
     1.1   History   3
     1.2   Purpose   3
     1.3   Rationale   3
     1.4   The method spectrum   4
     1.5   Composition   4
     1.6   Intended audience   5
     1.7   Constraints and assumptions   6

2   PRINCE2 overview   8

3   DSDM Atern overview   10

4   Advantages of using PRINCE2   12
     4.1   Business Case driven   12
     4.2   The Project Board   12
     4.3   Management by exception   12
     4.4   A start, middle and end   12
     4.5   Management stages   12
     4.6   Tolerances   13
     4.7   Product-based planning   13

     4.8   Time, cost and quality   13
     4.9   The Project Initiation Document   14
     4.10   Work Packages   14
     4.11   Project Assurance   14
     4.12   The quality path   14
     4.13   A de facto standard for all projects   15
     4.14   In summary   15

5   Advantages of using DSDM Atern   16
     5.1   Assessing the level of 'ceremony'   16
     5.2   The principles of DSDM Atern   16
     5.3   Flexing requirements   18
     5.4   Units, tens and hundreds – the UTH rule 19
     5.5   Communication before documentation   20
     5.6   MoSCoW (prioritisation)   20
     5.7   The Prioritised Requirements List   21
     5.8   Timeboxing   21
     5.9   Facilitated workshops   22
     5.10   Business involvement   22
     5.11   Iterative development   22
     5.12   Incremental delivery   22

6   Integrating PRINCE2 with DSDM
     Atern   24
     6.1   The fundamental synergy   24
     6.2   The specifics of integrating PRINCE2 with
            DSDM Atern   26
     6.3   Further adjustments to PRINCE2   27

PART 2 SPECIFIC GUIDANCE 31

7   The combined process model 33
   7.1   Representations of each process 33
   7.2   Mapping DSDM Atern to PRINCE2 during the controlled start 36
   7.3   Iterative and incremental product development 38
   7.4   The use of the eight PRINCE2 processes 39

8   The combined organisation structure 42
   8.1   The PRINCE2 Project Management Team – guidance 42
   8.2   DSDM Atern roles 44

9   The use of the PRINCE2 components 46
   9.1   Business Case 46
   9.2   Organisation 46
   9.3   Plans 47
   9.4   Controls 47
   9.5   Management of risk 49
   9.6   Quality in a project environment 50
   9.7   Configuration Management 51
   9.8   Change Control 51

10   The use of PRINCE2 and DSDM Atern techniques 53
   10.1   Timeboxing (DSDM Atern) 53
   10.2   Facilitated workshops (DSDM Atern) 55
   10.3   Iterative development and prototyping (DSDM Atern) 55
   10.4   Modelling (DSDM Atern) 56
   10.5   MoSCoW prioritisation (DSDM Atern) 56

   10.6   Product-based planning (PRINCE2) 57
   10.7   Quality review technique (PRINCE2) 57
   10.8   Change Control technique (PRINCE2) 58

PART 3 EXAMPLE AND CONCLUSION 59

11   Simple scenario 61
   11.1   The scenario 61
   11.2   Variations 65

12   Conclusion 68

PART 4 APPENDICES 71

Appendix A: Guidance on tailoring the PRINCE2 management products 73

Appendix B: Terminology used in DSDM v4.2 77

Appendix C: Further information 78
   PRINCE2 publications 78
   Useful links 78
   PRINCE2 accreditation 78

Appendix D: Glossaries 79
   DSDM glossary 79
   PRINCE2 glossary 81

Index 87

List of figures

Figure 1.1   Method spectrum diagram – typical characteristics

Figure 2.1   The processes and components of PRINCE2

Figure 3.1   The components of DSDM Atern

Figure 4.1   The TCQ triangle

Figure 5.1   Contrasting DSDM Atern with the traditional approach

Figure 5.2   A MoSCoW list

Figure 6.1   How PRINCE2 and DSDM Atern integrate when the methods are combined

Figure 7.1   The PRINCE2 process model

Figure 7.2   The DSDM Atern lifecycle

Figure 7.3   The Project Manager's perspective of the PRINCE2 processes

Figure 7.4   Work Packages within a management stage

Figure 7.5   Work Packages within a management stage delivered incrementally

Figure 7.6   Examples of Work Package contents

Figure 8.1   The combined organisational structure of PRINCE2 and DSDM Atern

Figure 10.1   How timeboxing levels can work with PRINCE2

Figure 11.1   The investigation–refinement–consolidation timebox

List of tables

Table 7.1   Mapping the DSDM Atern lifecycle onto PRINCE2

Table 7.2   Description of DSDM Atern products

Table 7.3   PRINCE2 processes

Table 11.1   Desired results for scenario after the investigation, refinement and consolidation cycles of the timebox

Table 11.2   Prioritised Requirements List for scenario after MoSCoW analysis

Table A.1   Suggested changes to the PRINCE2 management products

Table B.1   The nine principles of DSDM v4.2

Table B.2   The lifecycle phases of DSDM v4.2

Table B.3   The roles in DSDM v4.2

Acknowledgements

The Stationery Office (TSO) and the author, Keith Richards of Keith Richards Consulting, would like to thank the DSDM Consortium for their support and the following people for their help in putting together this publication:

Contributor

Maree Richards   RKEA

Reviewers

Graham Devine   Adjunct

David Hicks   RADTAC

Tony Levene   Quality Projects (Consulting) Limited

Brian Lyons   Number Six Software, Inc

Bruce McNaughton   Customer Driven Solutions Limited

Michael Mooney   Civil Nuclear Constabulary

Mik Quinlan   CIO Consulting Limited

Jennifer Stapleton   Outperform UK Limited

Susan Stevens   Maven Training

Paul Turner   Business & IS Skills Ltd

Tony Watts   Pearce Mayfield

Steve Wickham   WPM Group

Commissioning editor

Zoe Peden   TSO

Maturity mark

The TSO maturity mark on the back cover will help you decide if this publication is positioned at the appropriate level for your requirements and provide a route map to progress with embedding OGC guidance. This publication, *Agile Project Management: Running PRINCE2 projects with DSDM Atern*, is Level 3.

Level 3 is Defined (institutionalised), which means that the OGC guidance is defined/confirmed as a standard business process.

For more information on the TSO maturity mark and how it can help you please visit www.best-management-practice.com

Part 1
Rationale for integration

1 Introduction

1.1 HISTORY

PRINCE2 represents one of the most significant advances to project management in recent years. By 2002 PRINCE2 had become firmly established as the preferred method of choice for projects throughout the UK and Europe. Currently PRINCE2 is internationally recognised, with examinations in PRINCE2 having taken place in 56 countries, and it is available in 15 languages.

Dynamic Systems Development Method (DSDM) was created in 1995 in order to find a balance between large prescriptive methods and a culture of informal working in software development. Since its inception it has had nearly 1000 members, who have helped to build the method collaboratively. In 2002 it was recognised as one of the most established methods to join the Agile Alliance, an organisation which has set a global standard for agile software development. In 2007 DSDM released a new 'free to view, free to use' version called Atern, which can now be applied to any type of project in any environment.

However, despite the existence of these two methods, the rates of failure and dissatisfaction with the outcomes of projects are still surprisingly high. Even more so when it could be argued that 'projects' have been taking place since the time of the pyramids and Stonehenge!

1.2 PURPOSE

The purpose of this publication is to provide a summary on how to integrate the two approaches of PRINCE2 and DSDM Atern. Further to explaining how to integrate PRINCE2 and DSDM Atern, the publication explains the reasoning behind it so that individuals will understand what to do and why to do it.

In general terms, integrating PRINCE2 and DSDM Atern involves combining a method for project management with a method for project delivery. It is also the case that it blends a traditional style of thinking with a new agile mindset.

This integration will be described at a general level in terms of how the two have many synergies, and at the detailed level where the mechanics of the integration are examined for each process, component, technique and management product of PRINCE2.

1.3 RATIONALE

The reason for integrating PRINCE2 and DSDM Atern is that as a whole they can be more effective than they are separately. There is a golden rule in life that 'if it ain't broke, don't try and fix it', so is there really a need to enhance PRINCE2 by looking at how to integrate it with DSDM Atern?

The short answer is yes. The method arena is always moving on and there is currently strong interest in the concept of agile projects and agile project management. In today's marketplace there are ever growing demands on organisations to execute projects which deliver the right thing at the right time and at the right price, but we are still a long way from making this 'business as usual'.

Both PRINCE2 and DSDM Atern are well-established approaches in their own fields and when they are combined they can address the needs of a much wider range of projects in order to deliver more benefits to the business. Integrating the two together can give an organisation more flexibility and choice when deciding how to run a project. If individuals within the organisation are empowered, they have the freedom to decide what blend is 'fit for purpose' in any given situation, thereby increasing their chances of a successful project.

1.4 THE METHOD SPECTRUM

There are several methods available in the project management marketplace at present. Each one positions itself (or is positioned) along a spectrum which could be described as ranging from 'traditional' to 'agile'.

Where to place PRINCE2 and DSDM Atern on this spectrum would depend on how each method was being used by an organisation, but PRINCE2 is seen as being towards the traditional end of the spectrum and DSDM Atern as being in the centre or towards the agile end.

Broadly speaking, traditional projects are seen as being structured, heavyweight, sequential and largely document driven with the need for distinct sign-offs at specific points. These sign-offs can sometimes have a reputation for being unalterable. At the other end of the scale, agile projects are regarded as unstructured, lightweight, iterative, collaborative and responsive to change.

These two extremes do not in themselves represent good or bad, merely a choice. The choice will depend on the needs of the project.

More accurately the choice between traditional and agile approaches can be further subdivided into three areas: predictive, convergent and emergent.

Diagrammatically the typical characteristics are shown in Figure 1.1, where the centre and right columns would be classed as agile.

It is important to note that different methods can be appropriate to different situations and it is important that the correct method or method blend is used at the right time. A lot depends on the volatility of the product being delivered or the technical environment. If it is very well understood and unlikely to change during the course of

the project then a predictive approach can be used (e.g. a simple road bridge). On the other hand, if the product being delivered is not yet fully understood, this may favour a more emergent approach (e.g. a new product for the computer games market).

It is also important to understand that although each method has a natural tendency or a particular set of characteristics this does not mean that it has to work in that way.

PRINCE2 has been designed to work on any project and one of the ways it achieves this is by being scalable and tailorable. Therefore making adjustments to PRINCE2 which are already built in could move it away from the left-hand side of the method spectrum.

How far depends on what is already in PRINCE2 and what can be added to it without compromising any of its strengths. This will be explored in the coming pages.

DSDM Atern is normally positioned as convergent, but it is equally comfortable when being run in an emergent style.

1.5 COMPOSITION

The publication is divided into three parts. Part 1 (Chapters 1–6) brings together the rationale for integrating PRINCE2 with DSDM Atern. In order to do this the fundamentals of each approach are summarised. Then the most important characteristics of PRINCE2 and DSDM Atern are highlighted and explained. This is done separately in order to explore fully why each method has become a de facto standard in its own right. Part 1 concludes by explaining the advantages of combining the two methods as their respective strengths often counterbalance any specific shortcomings.

Part 2 (Chapters 7–10) moves from the theory discussed in Part 1 to the practicalities of being able to execute this. Each chapter in Part 2 will describe in specific detail what needs to be done when integrating PRINCE2 and DSDM

Figure 1.1 Method spectrum diagram – typical characteristics

Predictive	Convergent	Emergent
• A lot of work is done at the start – sometimes called BDUF (Big Design Up-Front) • Lots of early detail where possible • Sequential • Document driven • Closely controlled change	• Some work is done at the start – sometime called EDUF (Enough Design Up-Front) • Moderate level of detail is baselined early • Sequential and iterative • Lean documentation and informal communication • Happy to accommodate change	• Very little work is done at the start – sometimes called No DUF (No Design Up-Front) • Very little detail at the outset • Iterative • Communication by interaction of individuals • Embraces constant change

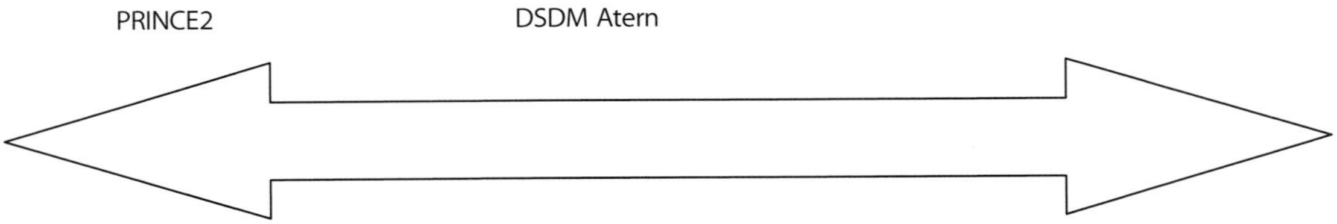

PRINCE2　　　　　　DSDM Atern

Atern together. This covers how the process model and the organisation structures should look. Each PRINCE2 component is assessed and guidance is given on how to use them appropriately. DSDM Atern techniques are then examined and the way they should be deployed on a PRINCE2 project is described.

Part 3 (Chapters 11–12) provides a walkthrough of a simple example to show how DSDM Atern could work when integrating PRINCE2 and DSDM Atern. Following this there is a conclusion to the theory and the practicalities of this integration.

Part 4 contains three appendices covering aspects such as specific management Product Description changes, a glossary, and information about mapping to the previous version of DSDM.

1.6 INTENDED AUDIENCE

This publication is aimed primarily at two audiences. First, it is for people directly involved in projects such as Project Managers and Project Support who wish to take their expertise and knowledge to a new level. Running PRINCE2 projects using DSDM Atern gives project teams a different angle on how to execute a project. In certain circumstances it may be the only way to run a project – there may be no viable alternative.

Second, it is aimed at people who are responsible for supporting strategic thinking and directing the delivery of benefits to the business. These people would typically sit at programme or programme support level and would be responsible for evaluating the approaches an organisation uses such as their choice of project management methods and tools.

The publication should also prove useful to many other disciplines. The concept and the realities of running traditional style methods with an agile flavour is thought by many to be at the leading edge of thinking in the methods arena. Therefore this text may prove of interest to methodologists and academics alike.

1.7 CONSTRAINTS AND ASSUMPTIONS

1.7.1 Style

The text has been written in a style that brings the two methods together by looking at their respective strengths and limitations. This often results in contrasting PRINCE2 with DSDM Atern and picking the best option from each.

Often there is little need to explain how to integrate certain areas of the two methods – it can simply be a case of use this from PRINCE2 and use that from DSDM Atern. When this is the case the text seeks to explain the advantage of a particular choice and why it has been chosen.

There are occasions when it is necessary to explain how to integrate parts of each method and when this happens it will be supported by a more detailed exposition.

This publication does not intend to provide detailed information about either PRINCE2 or DSDM Atern as this would duplicate existing text in either of the two reference

manuals that describe each method in detail. However, a summary of each approach is included in Part 1.

The publication aims to help bring the two approaches together from a PRINCE2 perspective and it is assumed that the reader would have access to the PRINCE2 manual *Managing Successful Projects with PRINCE2* (OGC 2005). Although the manual will still prove useful, it has not been written for DSDM organisations that are planning to adopt PRINCE2.

1.7.2 Implementation shortcomings

The aim of the publication is to describe how and why to integrate PRINCE2 and DSDM Atern and this description is achieved by contrasting the relative merits of each method. It is often the case that where PRINCE2 has limitations DSDM Atern can add value, and vice versa.

It is therefore important not to confuse a limitation of either method with a poor implementation of each method.

An example of this is documentation. Either method could be implemented poorly by producing either too much or too little documentation. This would not be an inherent fault of either method, just a case of poor implementation.

However, there are common tendencies with each method as well as common implementation problems, and it is the former which this publication seeks to explore, not the latter.

It is not uncommon for PRINCE2 documentation to be implemented in an overly bureaucratic way. This is the most common mistake when implementing PRINCE2, although there are countless examples of PRINCE2 being implemented without enough documentation.

The opposite is the case with DSDM Atern. The most common mistake is to implement it without enough documentation. Again, there are countless examples of

DSDM Atern being implemented with too much documentation.

The previous two paragraphs illustrate implementation problems, although it should be noted that PRINCE2 will typically have more documentation than DSDM Atern due to the fundamentals of each method. Organisational culture may also have an effect here: a large pharmaceutical company would typically have more project documentation than a medium-sized software house.

1.7.3 Audience knowledge

The text has been written with the assumption that the reader is familiar with PRINCE2. It is presumed that they have been involved with PRINCE2 projects and may be qualified to PRINCE2 Foundation level. Certain sections are written for PRINCE2 'experts' who would typically have had a lot of experience of PRINCE2 projects, particularly from the project management perspective. They may be qualified at PRINCE2 practitioner level.

No prior knowledge of agile methods such as DSDM Atern is required although being qualified to DSDM Foundation level would be an advantage when trying to understand the more advanced concepts which are aimed at the expert level.

1.7.4 Use of the term 'method'

The term 'method' has a wide range of interpretations throughout project management and in other areas such as science, music and art. In this publication the term 'method' will be used to describe a collection of processes, techniques, structures and principles, which all sit within an overarching philosophy.

Depending on individual usage, 'method' can be seen as synonymous with such words as 'methodology', 'approach' and 'framework'. Throughout the text the word 'method' will be used to cover all of these. This is in keeping with the PRINCE2 definition and usage throughout the PRINCE2 manual, although DSDM Atern literature often uses the terms 'framework' and 'approach'.

1.7.5 Versions

The text has been written using the fourth edition of the PRINCE2 manual entitled *Managing Successful Projects with PRINCE2* (OGC 2005).

It is also possible to use this publication with the third edition of the PRINCE2 manual, although some minor allowances would need to be made. It would not be advisable to use this publication with the first or second editions.

From the DSDM perspective this publication can be used with DSDM version 4.2 or DSDM Atern. Any significant differences are noted at the relevant point in the text.

It would not be advisable to use this publication with DSDM version 3 or earlier.

2   PRINCE2 overview

PRINCE2 is a structured method for effective project management. PRINCE stands for PRoject IN Controlled Environments and was first established in 1989 by the Central Computer and Telecommunications Agency (CCTA). PRINCE was preceded by PROMPTII in the 1970s, which was adopted by UK government as the standard for all information system projects.

PRINCE2 was launched in 1996 to provide guidance on all projects and not just for information systems. It has now become a de facto standard used extensively by the UK government, the private sector and internationally.

PRINCE2 is based on the principles of good project management, which are:

- A project is finite with a definite start and end.
- Projects always need to be managed in order to be successful.
- All parties in a project need to be clear about why the project is needed, what it is intended to achieve, how it will achieve it and what their responsibilities are in that achievement.

PRINCE2 aims to help organisations by providing a common approach to the way they address business change and to be aware of the benefits that having a common approach can provide.

Projects may exist in their own right, have relationships with other projects or be part of a larger programme. PRINCE2 is flexible and scalable and can be applied in all of these situations.

PRINCE2 provides organisations with:

- Controlled management of change from an investment perspective

- Active involvement of stakeholders throughout the project
- An approach to distinguish between the management of the project and the development of the product(s) so that it can be applied to any project.

PRINCE2 provides projects with:

- A controlled and organised start, middle and end
- Regular reviews of progress against plan and against the Business Case
- Flexible decision points
- Automatic management control of any deviations from the plan
- The involvement of management and stakeholders at the right time during the project
- Good communication channels between the Project Management Team and the rest of the organisation
- Agreement on the required quality at the outset and continuous monitoring against those requirements.

Project Managers using PRINCE2 are able to:

- Establish terms of reference as a prerequisite to the start of a project
- Use a defined structure for delegation, authority and communication
- Divide the project into manageable stages for more accurate planning
- Ensure that resource commitment from management is part of any approval to proceed
- Provide regular but brief management reports
- Keep meetings with management and stakeholders to a minimum but at the vital points in the project.

People who will be using the products created are able to:

- Participate in all the decision-making on a project

- If desired, be fully involved in day-to-day progress
- Participate in quality checks throughout the project
- Ensure that their requirements are being adequately satisfied.

PRINCE2 uses 'management by exception' for the senior management of the project. This is an event driven concept, which ensures that interventions are made only when necessary. This allows the Project Manager to continue with the job unless something is forecast to go wrong. Senior management is kept fully informed about the project without the need to attend meetings frequently.

PRINCE2 does not cover all subjects relevant to project management because tools and techniques can vary between projects and organisations. Certain aspects of project management are covered by existing and proven methods and are therefore excluded from PRINCE2.

Examples of these are:

- People management techniques such as motivation, delegation and team leadership
- Generic planning techniques such as Gantt charts and critical path analysis
- The creation and management of corporate quality management and quality assurance mechanisms
- Budgetary control and earned value analysis techniques.

Figure 2.1 shows the processes and components of PRINCE2.

PRINCE2 comprises:

- 8 processes
- 8 components
- 3 techniques
- 36 management Product Descriptions
- 10 project management role descriptions.

Figure 2.1 The processes and components of PRINCE2

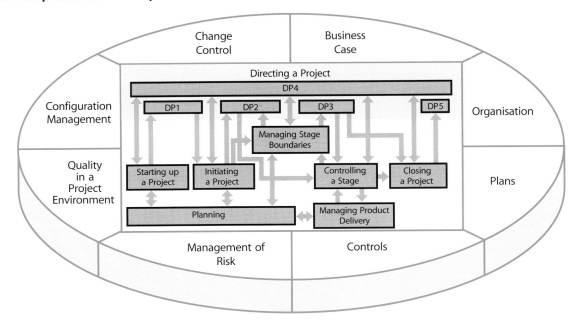

3 DSDM Atern overview

DSDM Atern is an approach which is derived from the current best practices for project management and product delivery as experienced by the members of the DSDM Consortium. The DSDM Consortium owns the method and is a not for profit membership organisation that continually promotes and improves the method by collaboratively involving its membership.

The DSDM Consortium was founded in 1995 and produced the first version of the method to a largely UK-based audience. Since then it has evolved in response to the changing climate of business change and the ever-increasing demands on how this change is delivered. It has now become internationally accepted as a leading agile method and perhaps the most recognised approach to agile project management and product delivery.

As with PRINCE2, DSDM was originally created for information systems projects. However, it was soon being used on a variety of business-only projects and the later versions of DSDM can be applied to any project. The name DSDM stands for 'dynamic systems development method', although nowadays it is used for much more than just software development and is commonly known as simply 'DSDM' or 'Atern'.

DSDM Atern focuses on the priorities of the business and ensures that products are delivered safely within the required quality, time and cost constraints of the project. DSDM Atern harnesses the knowledge, experience and creativity of the people who will be using the solution as well as those who are developing it. This takes place throughout the project by using an iterative lifecycle to evolve the most appropriate solution to satisfy the objectives of the project.

DSDM Atern puts a strong emphasis on the need to deliver a timely solution while at the same time maintaining the appropriate level of quality. DSDM Atern achieves this by delivering solutions that:

- Satisfy the real requirements of business, in a business driven order of importance
- Support the way the business needs to work
- Are delivered on time and within budget
- Are delivered quickly, and yet are robust and right
- Are delivered incrementally in useful chunks, with a business focus in order to gain an early return on investment.

DSDM Atern comprises a philosophy and a set of principles. These are supported by a process with a flexibly defined set of products. For the people on the project there are a flexibly defined set of roles and responsibilities. Guidance is given on practices and techniques, which is experience based, enabling them to be applied in the most appropriate way to any project.

Figure 3.1 shows the components of DSDM Atern.

Figure 3.1 The components of DSDM Atern

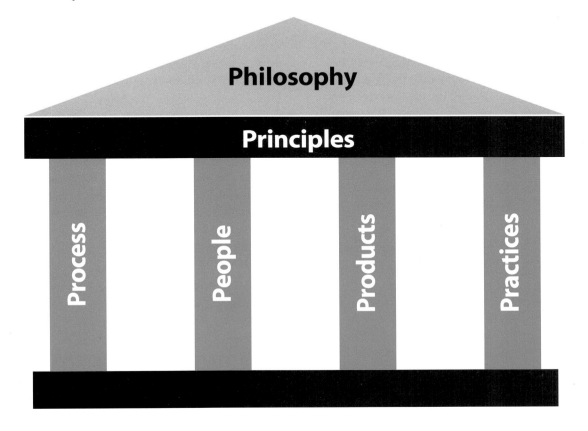

4 Advantages of using PRINCE2

Before looking at ways of integrating PRINCE2 with DSDM Atern, this chapter will outline the strengths of PRINCE2 and particularly highlight the elements that differentiate it from other approaches. In this way it can be seen what PRINCE2 does irrespective of whether or not it is being run in tandem with another method. It is important not to lose these strengths when integrating PRINCE2 with DSDM Atern.

The advantages of using DSDM Atern will be described in a similar way in the next chapter.

4.1 BUSINESS CASE DRIVEN

PRINCE2 regards the Business Case as a project's most important set of information. This creates the opportunity for a failing project to be stopped at the earliest possible moment. In the real world this is not always seen as a good sign when a lot of money and resources have already been committed, but the principle of letting the Business Case drive the project is a sound one.

What is more likely than a Business Case not being viable on a project is that the Business Case on a project has become marginal in relation to another project which has not started. This is where the Business Case driven approach is again appropriate.

It also helps focus a project on the end result and not just the means of getting there.

4.2 THE PROJECT BOARD

Most projects adopt the concept of a group of strategically aligned people providing direction to the project. PRINCE2 refers to this as the Project Board. It enables a Project Manager to focus on managing the day-to-day running of a project in the knowledge that if necessary he or she can seek assistance from an established group of people who will be looking after the interests of the project from the perspective of a business, user or supplier.

4.3 MANAGEMENT BY EXCEPTION

A large part of the PRINCE2 method either supports, or is based around, the concept of management by exception. It allows the relationship between the Project Manager and the Project Board to operate in the most efficient way possible. PRINCE2 is almost completely event driven and this means that interventions are kept down to a minimum by correctly using management stages and stage tolerances.

To support this there need to be disciplines in place to ensure that the appropriate reporting (Highlight Reports) and Project Assurance are taking place.

4.4 A START, MIDDLE AND END

PRINCE2 breaks a project down into three distinct parts and provides processes to support each one. This helps clarify to those involved with a project that the project is finite and temporary. It also provides a clear framework to ensure that a project is correctly started before large amounts of resource are committed to it, and that when the project finishes it does so in a deliberate way and therefore avoids a common problem of drifting into operational use.

4.5 MANAGEMENT STAGES

One of the most important principles of PRINCE2 is the concept of using stages. More accurately, they are management stages (as opposed to technical stages) and it is vital to use these correctly if the PRINCE2 project is to be well run. However, control is often misapplied (or even not used) on projects because the importance of this 'fire break' to check the ongoing viability of a project is not understood. There are many important things that can be done at the end of a stage. The most important is to update and revisit the Business Case that drives a PRINCE2 project.

4.6 TOLERANCES

Another important control which is easily understood and easy to use is that of giving a management stage a tolerance. This is a permissible deviation from a plan and supports management by exception. Primarily this is focused on giving tolerance values for time and cost and allows the Project Manager a degree of freedom and empowerment in which to manage a stage.

Tolerance can also be used at project or Work Package level.

4.7 PRODUCT-BASED PLANNING

Even though this technique is classed as 'optional' by PRINCE2, it is central to all projects using the PRINCE2 method of project management. It is surprising how many projects that claim to use PRINCE2 do not use product-based planning. This powerful technique can seem counter-intuitive because there is a natural tendency to make a plan activity-based. However, a product-based approach is easier to project manage as it ensures that every activity contributes to a constituent product.

4.8 TIME, COST AND QUALITY

The fact that PRINCE2 is built around the traditional project management triangle of time, cost and quality (the TCQ triangle; Figure 4.1) is included in this chapter as a strength, although it does limit PRINCE2 in terms of other dimensions to this model such as scope.

Although PRINCE2 does not explicitly refer to the TCQ triangle (sometimes referred to as the 'iron triangle'), it is very hard to argue against the fact that it is built around this concept and therefore that it is in line with the commonly accepted fundamentals of project management.

The reason that the time, cost and quality triangle is a strength is that building PRINCE2 around these three key variables makes it very straightforward. The visibility of all three throughout the processes, components, techniques, management products and roles makes it clear to the Project Manager and those involved in the project how important it is to monitor and control these three variables, which will inevitably pull against each other.

Figure 4.1 The TCQ (time, cost, quality) triangle

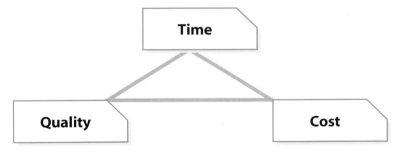

4.9 THE PROJECT INITIATION DOCUMENT

The Project Initiation Document (PID) is normally a collection of documents that have been built up over the controlled start and represents the basis for committing money and resources to the project. It also acts as the baseline against which progress and success can be measured.

The importance of the PID stems from the fact that it contains three essential management products – the Business Case, the Project Plan and the Risk Log – and that this information has evolved and been checked through the controlled start (by being part of the Project Mandate and Project Brief).

The PID acts as the gateway between the time when one is considering whether to do a project and the time when one has decided to do it. If used correctly the PID gets a project off to a sound start, possibly before a large amount of money and resources has been committed to it.

The PID also contains information about Project Approach, which can contain details about the use of DSDM Atern.

Unfortunately common mistakes are made when creating a PID, which result from a poor implementation of PRINCE2. It can happen that a large, 'unreadable' document is created, or people regard the PID as an end in itself and not a means to one. It is not uncommon for a PID to be produced in the belief that this is all PRINCE2 is!

4.10 WORK PACKAGES

A Work Package allows PRINCE2 to operate in any project situation where different teams or companies not using PRINCE2 are delivering products. The advantage to PRINCE2 of the Work Package is that it allows project management to be separated from product delivery. This will prove significant when combining PRINCE2 with DSDM Atern. The key to the success of a Work Package is in using the correct level of formality. This may be different if a team internal to an organisation is supplying the product.

4.11 PROJECT ASSURANCE

Project Assurance is another example of a concept that PRINCE2 brings to projects, which increases their likelihood of success but is often overlooked by organisations that have implemented PRINCE2. The Project Board can do this directly or by delegation. Either way, the use of a view independent of the Project Manager to act as a sanity check usually pays dividends. This operates more effectively when it is offered in the form of guidance as opposed to the action of an audit.

4.12 THE QUALITY PATH

A mantra often cited with PRINCE2 is that 'Quality is built in and not bolted on'. A lot of the PRINCE2 method concentrates on ensuring that the finished product and any sub-product is fit for purpose. Quality considerations permeate every area of PRINCE2, particularly those of Configuration Management, Change Control (issues), Quality Review Technique, the Product Description for specialist products and numerous Product Descriptions for management products.

The aim of PRINCE2 is to keep quality at the forefront of all areas of the project. This subject is addressed at the very beginning of the PRINCE2 process model, where the broad quality expectations of the customer are documented, and then continues throughout the project all the way down to the detailed quality criteria to be checked as part of managing product delivery.

4.13 A DE FACTO STANDARD FOR ALL PROJECTS

PRINCE2 has become an international standard and has been adopted by thousands of organisations worldwide. There is therefore a common language of communication for everyone involved in project management. This enables resources to transfer within or between organisations with a reduced learning curve for those involved.

Further to this PRINCE2 can be applied to any project in any environment (internal or external) in any organisation. It is also highly scalable and tailorable. Although its origins are found in the IT sector (PRINCE), it is now a generic approach (as is DSDM Atern).

4.14 IN SUMMARY

This chapter has outlined the significant strengths of PRINCE2 and represents many concepts that are considered to characterise best practice in project management today. When combining with DSDM Atern, these should remain in place and not be compromised.

5 Advantages of using DSDM Atern

Many organisations use DSDM Atern and it is common to find that this is the management method of choice, without the need to use any other method. The fact that DSDM Atern can exist in its own right and has been in existence for over a decade illustrates that it consists of practices that work when applied in the real world.

As with the previous chapter, these advantages will be looked at in isolation in order to identify clearly specific strengths that need to be preserved when combining DSDM Atern with PRINCE2.

5.1 ASSESSING THE LEVEL OF 'CEREMONY'

DSDM Atern has a pragmatic approach to how rigorously the method should be applied on a project. A project involving a co-located team of six people working on an in-house project for six weeks will require less rigour than a similar type of project involving 50 people working for six months in three different countries where half the team is from an external supplier.

To determine how much ceremony is required, DSDM Atern carries out a self-assessment of the project and specifically looks at the risks the method itself needs to deal with. As an example of this, DSDM Atern would assess that communication will be harder if the team is based in the UK and India rather than in the same room. DSDM Atern would therefore recommend that special attention would need to be given to the way the project team communicated in the first case.

Picking the correct level of rigour is important to increasing the chances of a successful project. Too much will ultimately stifle the project team and slow the project down, whereas not enough will lead to errors and result in the delivery of inaccurate products. A simple analogy is that of driving a car up a hill. The quickest and most efficient way to get to the top of the hill would be by selecting the correct gear. Too low a gear would be slow and inefficient whereas too high a gear could stall the car.

5.2 THE PRINCIPLES OF DSDM ATERN

The eight principles of DSDM Atern embody its agile ethos. When integrating PRINCE2 and DSDM Atern they create a powerful agile culture from within a strong layer of governance.

The eight principles support the overall philosophy of DSDM Atern. They are regarded as a mindset and represent the way you work. A summary of the eight principles is described below.

Principle 1: Focus on the business need

Every decision taken during a project should be viewed in the light of the overriding project goal, which is to deliver what the business needs it to deliver, when it needs to be delivered.

Always remember that a project is a means to an end, not an end in itself.

In order to fulfil this principle, DSDM Atern teams will:

- Establish an understanding of what the business really needs
- Understand the true business priorities
- Apply the 80:20 rule
- Seek continuous business sponsorship and commitment.

Principle 2: Deliver on time

Delivering products on time is a very desirable outcome for a project and is quite often the single most important success factor. Late delivery can undermine the very rationale for a project, especially where market opportunities or legal deadlines are involved.

In order to fulfil this principle, DSDM Atern teams will:

- Timebox the work
- Focus on business priorities
- Always hit deadlines.

Principle 3: Collaborate

Teams that work in a spirit of active cooperation and commitment will always outperform groups of individuals working only in loose association. Collaboration encourages increased understanding, greater speed and shared ownership, which enable teams to perform at a level that exceeds the sum of their parts.

In order to fulfil this principle, DSDM Atern teams will:

- Involve the right stakeholders, at the right time, throughout the project
- Ensure that the members of the team are empowered to take decisions on behalf of those they represent
- Actively involve the business representatives
- Build a one-team culture.

Principle 4: Never compromise quality

In DSDM Atern, the level of quality to be delivered should be agreed at the start. All work should be aimed at achieving that level of quality. No more and no less. A solution has to be 'good enough'. If the business agrees that the functionality in a minimum usable subset has been provided adequately, then it should be acceptable.

In order to fulfil this principle, DSDM Atern teams will:

- Set the level of quality at the outset
- Ensure that quality does not become a variable
- Design, document and test appropriately
- Build in quality by constant review
- Test early and continuously.

Principle 5: Develop iteratively

In order to converge on an accurate business solution DSDM Atern uses iterative development. The concept of iteration is embedded throughout DSDM Atern's lifecycle, down to the lowest level of timeboxing. It is very rare that anything is built perfectly first time and projects operate within a changing world. DSDM Atern advocates a pragmatic approach to change, which relies on iteration in order to embrace change and produce a better solution.

In order to fulfil this principle, DSDM Atern teams will:

- Be creative, experiment, learn and evolve
- Embrace change – the solution will evolve as the team learns more about it
- Take an iterative approach to building all products
- Continually confirm a correct solution is being built
- Converge on an accurate solution.

Principle 6: Build incrementally from firm foundations

In order to deliver real business benefit early, DSDM Atern advocates incremental development. This encourages stakeholder confidence and is a source of feedback for use in subsequent increments. Increments that are deployed into operational use may lead to early business benefit. DSDM Atern advocates first understanding the scope of the business problem to be solved and the proposed solution, but not so detailed that the project becomes paralysed.

In order to fulfil this principle, DSDM Atern teams will:

- Do enough design up front to create strong foundations
- Strive for early delivery of business benefit where possible
- Accept that most detail emerges later rather than sooner
- Evolve more precise estimates as the project progresses.

Principle 7: Communicate continuously and clearly

Poor communication is often cited as the biggest single cause of project failure. DSDM Atern techniques are specifically designed to improve communication effectiveness for teams and individuals.

In order to fulfil this principle, DSDM Atern teams will:

- Use facilitated workshops
- Use rich communication techniques such as modelling and prototyping
- Present iterations of the evolving solution early and often
- Keep documentation lean and timely
- Manage stakeholder expectations throughout the project
- Encourage informal, face-to-face communication at all levels.

Principle 8: Demonstrate control

It is essential to be in control of a project at all times. A DSDM Atern team needs to be proactive when monitoring and controlling progress in line with the foundations phase products, especially the Business Case. You need to be able to prove you are in control.

In order to fulfil this principle, DSDM Atern teams, especially the Project Manager and Team Leader, will:

- Use an appropriate level of formality
- Be able to demonstrate control at all times
- Make plans visible to appropriate stakeholders
- Measure progress through focus on delivery of products rather than completed activities
- Manage proactively
- Evaluate continuing project viability based on the business objectives.

5.3 FLEXING REQUIREMENTS

The single most important concept in DSDM Atern is that of managing the amount of product delivered in preference to flexing time, cost or quality. The term 'requirement' is synonymous with functionality, feature or scope and it is the focus on this that enables DSDM Atern to be classed as an agile method.

The advantage of concentrating on managing the features delivered on a project is that it is often the most natural way of working in today's commercial world where timescales and fitness for purpose are often the most important consideration for any business change.

Flexing requirements adds a fourth dimension to the traditionally established TCQ triangle: F for feature (or function) (Figure 5.1).

A DSDM Atern project concentrates on this additional variable by default. When deciding what should be varied and what should not, it regards *time* as something that should be fixed so that deadlines can be hit and dependencies met. It regards *quality* as sacred because correcting this later will either be expensive or impossible. It also regards cost (particularly in the form of increased resources) as of little help in a fast-moving agile environment. This is primarily because when extra resources take the form of people, these individuals will need to undergo a steep learning curve before becoming productive.

Therefore slightly reducing the feature set is by default the preferred option and this is normally the case on the vast majority of projects.

There is one area of concern when using this approach relating to the amount of the final product that may be left out in order to hit the deadline with a product of the correct level of quality. The concern is that a large amount of the final product will not be delivered. On a correctly managed DSDM Atern project this concern will not

Figure 5.1 Contrasting DSDM Atern with the traditional approach

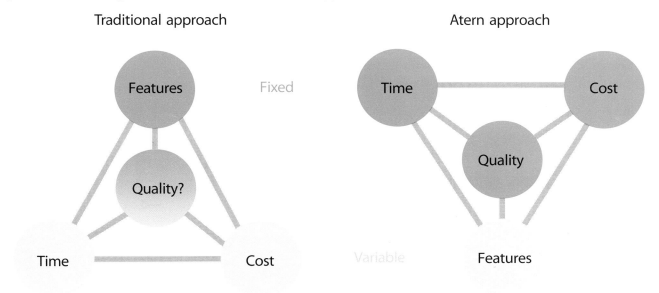

materialise unless estimates are so inaccurate that they are in effect meaningless. This would be a problem on any project.

Typically a project may need to drop between 5 and 10% of the originally envisaged feature set. It is important to point out that flexing requirements also permit the inclusion of new, perhaps more important, features, which can be added easily as new ideas or a greater understanding of the project occurs.

5.4 UNITS, TENS AND HUNDREDS – THE UTH RULE

A fundamental assumption on which DSDM Atern is built is that, although detail is important, it delays the production of any detailed definition of the requirements by baselining information at a higher level during the early part of a project.

The UTH rule is a guide (and not to be taken too literally) to the amount of requirements there will be at each point in a project:

- Very early on during the initial work you would probably be able to count the (high-level) requirements on the fingers of your hands.
- Shortly after this and after more investigation has moved the project further forward, the number of (medium level) requirements would have increased but it would still be less than a hundred.
- Finally, as the project fully defines the products in detail (low-level requirements), you may have hundreds of requirements although not thousands.

UTH stands for 'units, tens and hundreds', from elementary mathematics. Thousands are not included because if there were to be that many requirements it is likely that the project is so large it would need to be broken down into more than one project or run as a programme.

After each of the points within the project described above, DSDM Atern baselines the understanding of the requirements in order to check that the comprehension of the project as a whole is correct and, very importantly, to provide an appropriate estimate of the work involved.

These estimates represent a direct link with the level of detail of the requirements. As the understanding of the requirements increases and therefore so does the detail, then the accuracy of the estimates increases as well.

The way the requirements and their estimates evolve during a DSDM Atern project is underpinned by two beliefs. First, the definition of a project's requirements should not be detailed too early because it will almost certainly be inaccurate and it will be very difficult to estimate the amount of work involved using detailed requirements unless they have been captured at a more general level first.

The second belief is that early estimates will have a large margin of error and therefore any estimate made at this point should not be set too rigidly. A common mistake is that projects are held hostage to an initial estimate.

5.5 COMMUNICATION BEFORE DOCUMENTATION

Fundamental to DSDM Atern is that communication on a project should be performed in the most effective way possible. DSDM Atern calls this 'rich communication' and puts in place techniques and an ethos to make this happen.

DSDM Atern certainly does not advocate removing documentation from the project, but it does recommend making it as lean as possible by using other channels to complement it.

In most situations the written word is not the best way to get a message or an understanding from one person or group to another. A 35-page product specification is prone to misinterpretation, being out of date, containing jargon and perhaps not being fully read (if at all!). Even a simple e-mail can be read in several ways because there is no indication of the intended meaning of the person sending it.

DSDM Atern uses more interpersonal and visual systems in order to circumvent the problems with communicating primarily through documents.

People communicate more effectively when they can visualise their thoughts and interact face-to-face. The speed and the quality of two people discussing something while standing by a whiteboard far exceeds the same discussion held over the telephone. This in turn far exceeds the same discussion using e-mail.

Specific techniques to address this are modelling, facilitated workshops and prototyping (iterative development). DSDM Atern also creates a culture of rich communication by allowing a team to communicate informally – it is not always necessary to write everything down. However, this needs to be supported by a no blame culture in case a mistake is made. This culture is supported by the collaborate principle of DSDM Atern.

5.6 MoSCoW (PRIORITISATION)

DSDM Atern focuses on delivering the right product at the right time. In order to ensure that this happens it prioritises the products that are produced. DSDM Atern uses the MoSCoW technique for this. The basics of it are very easy to understand. In the term MoSCoW, 'M' stands for 'Must have', 'S' for 'Should have', 'C' for 'Could have' and 'W' for 'Won't have this time around' (see Figure 5.2).

The secret of success when using MoSCoW is to be sure that those requirements classed as a 'Must', really are.

Figure 5.2 A MoSCoW list

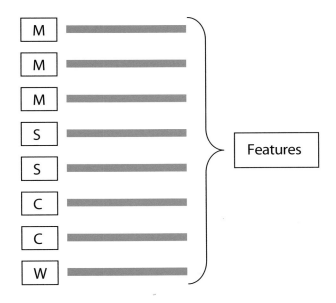

There is a natural tendency of business people to consider most things as 'Musts' when in reality they are not.

Two questions to ask in order to challenge the validity of a 'Must' are:

■ If this requirement is not delivered, would you want the rest of the solution?
■ Can this requirement be satisfied in another way?

If the answer to either question is yes, then the requirement is not a 'Must'.

This is another example of how DSDM Atern works in a natural way. When teams are faced with immovable deadlines the most effective way to achieve success is to prioritise and the MoSCoW technique is a user-friendly way of doing this.

It is important to use this technique proactively and throughout the project. Prioritisation in DSDM Atern is not the same as the last resort of very late descoping of a project.

5.7 THE PRIORITISED REQUIREMENTS LIST

Even on the smallest and most informal of DSDM Atern projects there will always be a Prioritised Requirements List (PRL). This product evolves throughout the project in line with the UTH rule and enables a project to be controlled using the MoSCoW technique. It is often the centre of attention on a DSDM Atern project and helps with managing the project. It is important to have the right level of granularity in the PRL at the right time. An example of this is that during the very early part of a project only the content of the PRL needs to be at a high level.

One advantage of the PRL is that it can be used to show the project status to the team and any other stakeholders by illustrating which features have been ticked off and which have not.

5.8 TIMEBOXING

The timeboxing technique is crucial to keeping a DSDM Atern project under control. Many parts of DSDM Atern support the iterative nature of product development and timeboxing removes the potential to over-engineer and procrastinate over any products.

This technique represents one of the hallmarks of an agile approach as it delivers the 'on-time' ethos of Principle 2 of DSDM Atern. This mindset applies equally to a timebox of two weeks or two months.

It is usually a difficult technique to master initially and the classic mistake is to extend a timebox when in difficulties as opposed to reducing the content of the timebox. It is very important that if a timebox is not going to achieve its objective in time, it needs be treated as a failed timebox, because this failure is indicating that estimates are incorrect and that corrective action is needed.

5.9 FACILITATED WORKSHOPS

Speed and a very rich level of communication are two advantages of a well-run workshop which has been independently facilitated. Facilitation is a core skill needed for a DSDM Atern project, because a well-run workshop usually requires someone who is neutral to keep control of the workshop process and the group dynamics, while letting the workshop participants produce the content.

An example of how a facilitator can help with the workshop process is by ensuring that the participants remain focused on the workshop objective and do not go off at a tangent or become stuck on one particular issue.

A facilitator would have several tools and techniques which could be employed to overcome individuals dominating proceedings or participants who are unable to contribute freely.

A final advantage of the workshop approach is that it creates a high level of ownership of the final outcome.

5.10 BUSINESS INVOLVEMENT

A strength of DSDM Atern is the focus it places on the business side of any project. The method regards a project as something which is being run *with* the business as opposed to *for* the business. To support this it has five clearly defined business roles, two of which are part of the core team responsible for product delivery (Business Ambassador and Business Analyst).

This business focus results in a greater level of ownership of the delivered solution. It also shortens communication lines and results in the rapid resolution of questions and problems. The chances of the final product being fit for

purpose are also greatly increased because members of the team are getting their information first hand.

5.11 ITERATIVE DEVELOPMENT

To be classed as an agile method it is necessary to support iterative development explicitly. The desire to think and work iteratively is based on the assumption that project teams will know a lot, but they won't know everything. This can be taken a step further by suggesting that project teams are more than happy that they don't fully understand the detailed nature of the problem. This allows them to experiment and investigate. This is sometimes referred to as prototyping.

Timeboxing will prevent iteration from being over-creative and the guidance in DSDM Atern advises that the normal cycle of iterative development of any product would be finished within three iterations. Configuration Management is also essential in order to stay in control.

This part of DSDM Atern directly contributes to the convergent position DSDM Atern has on the method spectrum mentioned in Chapter 1. Using this approach DSDM Atern endeavours to converge on a more accurate solution by communicating and checking the current level of understanding.

5.12 INCREMENTAL DELIVERY

Another feature of an agile method is incremental delivery where partial deliveries of the final product are made as early as possible if they are of benefit to the business. The opposite of this would be one, waterfall like, delivery at the end of a project.

An advantage of incremental delivery in DSDM Atern is that it gives early feedback to the project. There is no better feedback than when an interim product goes live and this can be used to improve the development of the rest of the final product. This is often seen as helping to reduce risk on a project.

Another benefit of incremental delivery is that it can provide an early return on investment (ROI), which can often be used to finance the rest of the project. In certain circumstances there may only be a viable Business Case if the project is delivered incrementally.

Other advantages include the ease of moving the product into service. This can be done in smaller, easier-to-manage chunks, which can ease the impact on such things as training and support.

6 Integrating PRINCE2 with DSDM Atern

This chapter looks at the reasoning behind integrating PRINCE2 with DSDM Atern, and then goes on to describe the specifics. The previous two chapters have highlighted their respective strengths and subsequent chapters will give a detailed account of what to do. This chapter explains why.

6.1 THE FUNDAMENTAL SYNERGY

As previously outlined, both methods have their own strengths and unique ways of working. It is not necessarily the case that combining them will create a situation where the whole is greater than the sum of its parts.

In order for a combined approach to work there needs to be similarity in certain areas and differences in others. An example of where similarity is needed is in the use of Product Descriptions – a combined approach would not work if one approach advocates using them and the other approach advocates not using them! An example of where difference is important is timeboxing – if PRINCE2 already used this technique there would be little added value in integrating the two methods.

In the most important areas PRINCE2 and DSDM Atern are similar where they need to be and different where they need to be.

6.1.1 Similarities

PRINCE2 and DSDM Atern are commonly described as 'coming from the same stable'. In the mid-1990s when DSDM Atern was being developed, the large number of people who developed it did so with PRINCE and PRINCE2 in mind. Therefore there is common ground on the importance of the Business Case, a product-based approach and business engagement.

The mechanics of both methods have similarities, too, in that they both possess a defined process model (or lifecycle) and Product Descriptions for each stage or phase of the project. They both define roles, responsibilities and team structures as well.

6.1.2 Differences

Although they have similar origins, they are not identical and there are two significant differences between PRINCE2 and DSDM Atern, which will ultimately lead to an ideal union when combining the two together:

- PRINCE2 focuses solely on project management whereas DSDM Atern does not. The DSDM Atern approach integrates project management disciplines with project delivery disciplines.
- DSDM Atern is seen as 'agile' whereas PRINCE2 is not.

6.1.2.1 Delivery

PRINCE2 explains what you need to do for effective project management. It provides processes and components, which creates a layer of project governance. PRINCE2 is very strong in this area and when combining with DSDM Atern this will remain in place. DSDM Atern also has guidance for project management, but it goes a step further than PRINCE2 by also providing guidance and techniques on how to do it.

6.1.2.2 Agility

Most people perceive PRINCE2 to be a traditional heavyweight project management method. This is unfortunate because the PRINCE2 manual contains extensive guidance on how to scale and tailor the PRINCE2 method. PRINCE2 projects can be run with a very light touch, but still contain the appropriate level of governance. However, perceptions are often taken as reality and although PRINCE2 can be used in a more agile way, there are still some fundamental agile concepts that are not explicitly or implicitly provided by PRINCE2.

6.1.2.3 Agile project management and delivery

Therefore in simple terms, by combining the two methods – which are similar in their mechanics – we can create an integrated approach, which not only covers the management and the delivery of a project, but also allows

the option to execute the project in an agile way. This is illustrated in Figure 6.1.

Figure 6.1 illustrates the integration of the two methods throughout the life of a project. IP is shown as larger than SU because more work will be taking place. SB (Managing Stage Boundaries) is not shown for reasons of clarity. PRINCE2 would be used for project governance and project management. There is an overlap with DSDM Atern concerning project management and this is shown where the colours merge. DSDM Atern would be used for product delivery.

Figure 6.1 How PRINCE2 and DSDM Atern integrate when the methods are combined

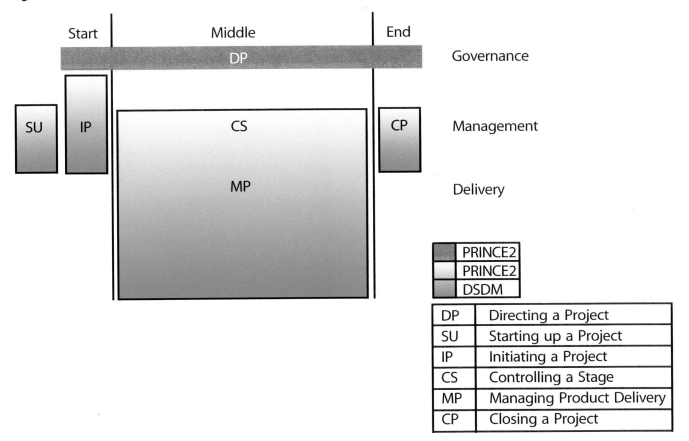

DP	Directing a Project
SU	Starting up a Project
IP	Initiating a Project
CS	Controlling a Stage
MP	Managing Product Delivery
CP	Closing a Project

6.2 THE SPECIFICS OF INTEGRATING PRINCE2 WITH DSDM ATERN

In order to explore the rationale for integrating PRINCE2 with DSDM Atern in more detail it is important to describe any limitations with PRINCE2 and how DSDM Atern would address them. As discussed in Chapter 4, PRINCE2 has many strengths, which must not be watered down or lost, but to move PRINCE2 from a method of governance to an agile project delivery method it is necessary to integrate or attach elements from DSDM Atern.

6.2.1 Reducing the heavyweight perception

Being perceived as a heavyweight method represents an Achilles heel for PRINCE2, which is unfortunate because it need not be the case.

Heavyweight approaches to a project are typified by a linear sequential process model with distinct sign-offs at the end of each phase. It is inflexible by nature and does not support iteration. At its worst it can be regarded as a 'waterfall approach'.

The following adjustments are needed to remove this perception.

6.2.1.1 Avoid too much bureaucracy and driving the process with documents

PRINCE2 can have a reputation for being bureaucratic and document heavy. Introducing the DSDM Atern ethos and DSDM Atern techniques can move PRINCE2 to a much more agile way of working. DSDM Atern shifts a lot of the communication traffic onto different channels such as models and informality (see section 5.5).

Document-driven processes on complex projects are inefficient if they are used as the primary channel of communication. Put simply, people stop (or cut down on) talking to each other and the focus of an individual becomes the creation of a document as opposed to the creation of a greater understanding.

It is often the case that this focus on the creation of a document turns into a defensive exercise where there is a conscious or perhaps subconscious desire to avoid getting blamed if a part of the project fails. In a document-driven culture many documents are written from the point of view of protecting an individual as opposed to the real reason for writing a document, which is to communicate understanding from one person or group of people to another.

6.2.1.2 Introduce iteration

The PRINCE2 process model does not explicitly or implicitly support the concept of iterative product development. Integrating PRINCE2 with DSDM Atern moves PRINCE2 from a predictive culture to a convergent one by fostering an attitude that iteration is good and is more likely to result in a greater understanding and a more beneficial product being delivered.

This iterative way of working occurs throughout a project and can apply to one piece of work on one day or a collection of products over a period of several months. It not only applies to the products being delivered, but also to the technical understanding of the solution and the definition of the business problem.

On any project there is normally a degree of iteration at Work Package level that may well be true iterative development, but it is more likely that this is rework, which is not the same thing. Iteration deliberately promotes investigation and clarification.

6.2.1.3 Become more receptive to change

Generally PRINCE2 does not regard change as a particularly positive thing. The tone of the PRINCE2 manual sees changes as events that 'can potentially ruin a project unless they are carefully controlled'. There is undoubtedly the need for control, but it is also true that not making a change could potentially ruin a project. Therefore the need to be adaptable and dynamic is highly desirable and is a feature of agile project management and delivery.

Many of the structures of DSDM Atern support this idea of being receptive to change (flexing requirements, the UTH rule and business involvement) and seeing it in a positive light because it will normally mean that a more beneficial product is being delivered.

Change is inevitable on a project. There are changes that result from the project being poorly defined at the outset and there are other changes that result from a greater understanding of the detailed nature of the project. There are also changes that result from factors which are external to the project.

The DSDM Atern approach to baselining (the UTH rule) and the initial phases of the DSDM Atern lifecycle aim to ensure that the project is well defined and that the only type of change is to the depth of the scope as opposed to the breadth. A correctly executed DSDM Atern project should not encounter the common problem of high-level 'scope creep' or 'moving goalposts'.

6.2.1.4 Baseline understanding before going into detail

PRINCE2 does this to a degree with the use of the controlled start to a project. This encompasses Starting up a Project (SU) and Initiating a Project (IP), which produce the Project Brief and the Project Initiation Document (PID), respectively. To avoid the heavyweight perception it is important to understand where to stop the development of these documents in order to avoid being too predictive.

DSDM Atern stops at a higher level in order to check that the project is going in the right direction in terms of the intended products being delivered and the viability of the project. It then starts to build partial versions of the

products early to clarify this further. This would involve using the exploration and engineering phases in DSDM Atern.

This is not explicitly covered by the PRINCE2 process model because to carry out this early work on the products will involve the use of specialists in receipt of Work Packages, which would normally be covered by the controlled middle of a PRINCE2 project and not the controlled start.

How far to take the PID in terms of detail is covered further in Chapter 7, where a preferred mapping is discussed and the importance of introducing some of the products from the foundations phase of the DSDM Atern lifecycle to be run in conjunction with IP is explained.

6.3 FURTHER ADJUSTMENTS TO PRINCE2

The advantages discussed so far have all been to do with removing the heavyweight perception that PRINCE2 often has. The effect of these adjustments is to make PRINCE2 look and feel more agile. However, to be fully agile PRINCE2 needs further adjustments, as described below.

6.3.1 Introduce the mechanisms to manage scope

As mentioned in Chapter 4, there are many excellent features which have enabled PRINCE2 to become a de facto standard for project management, but it does have one specific limitation in that it does not handle a project which is only using scope for tolerance (as opposed to the standard elements of time and cost). The need to be responsive to the features being delivered on a project is an essential ingredient of a method that wants to be seen as agile.

It could be argued that wanting to appear agile is not the primary reason for using scope for tolerance. The reality for most projects is that time and cost need to be fixed because it is either highly desirable to do so or there is quite simply no choice – the deadline is immovable and there is no more money or resources.

The PRINCE2 manual does mention using scope tolerance as a control, but only very briefly and there is no mention of any mechanics to support the concept, e.g. management products.

PRINCE2 is written from the traditional project viewpoint, where the most important variables to control are time, cost and quality (T, C and Q), whereas DSDM Atern would add functionality (or features) to this. Throughout the manual, and in particular the PRINCE2 management products, the focus is on T, C and Q with very little specific reference to scope.

When integrating PRINCE2 with DSDM Atern the scope of a project can be managed by using the Prioritised Requirements List (PRL) from DSDM Atern. This needs to be complemented by the involvement of the business at all levels of the project and by the timeboxing technique from DSDM Atern to ensure that prioritisation focuses on the timely delivery of products.

When managing the scope of a project it is important that the features being dropped or added are of the correct granularity. The UTH rule facilitates this by describing the features in such a way that they are not at too high a level (that they must exist in some form) or too low a level (that the time or cost saving would be negligible).

Change Control when managing scope needs to be dynamic. Significant changes or movement in the boundaries of the scope (scope creep) would need to be escalated formally. However, the project team should handle changes to the detail of the scope much more informally; it is working closely with the detail and will have the greatest understanding of the impact of the changes.

6.3.2 Create team structures at the product delivery level

PRINCE2 is a project management method and therefore team structures at the product delivery level are deliberately missing, apart from the use of a Team Manager role, which acts as a point of contact for the Project Manager.

DSDM Atern does cover product delivery and therefore integrating PRINCE2 with DSDM Atern enables there to be a set of roles that will enable projects to be run in a more agile way. A lot of the agility on a project is in the area of product delivery and therefore these roles are needed to support it.

It is important that these product delivery roles represent the business interest on the project. PRINCE2 has the Senior User role(s) and there may be delegated Project Assurance to support this. However, there is nothing below this and the business focused roles from DSDM Atern fit in underneath at the team level.

A similar situation exists for the Senior Supplier, where DSDM Atern has defined roles for the technical perspective of the project to fit in at the lower level.

Integrating the product delivery structures of DSDM Atern with the existing Project Management Team creates a more dynamic and quicker set of communication channels over the interface between the PRINCE2 Project Manager and the teams delivering the product.

6.3.3 Use techniques to enable product delivery

Integrating PRINCE2 with DSDM Atern automatically brings in a handful of techniques which directly help with product delivery. PRINCE2 deliberately avoids this. The advantages of facilitated workshops, timeboxing and MoSCoW are described in Chapter 5. Prototyping and modelling can help in creating products and may be Work Packages in their own right.

Having the option of using any of these five techniques gives PRINCE2 a closer link to product delivery, which is desirable to have when working in an agile way.

DSDM Atern explains how to use these techniques, when to use them and why they should be used.

The result of these techniques is to increase the visibility, collaboration, ownership and quality of the communication lines which are all essential to enable agile project management.

Part 2
Specific guidance

2

7 The combined process model

This chapter provides guidance on how to combine the PRINCE2 process model with the DSDM Atern lifecycle. Although the PRINCE2 manual uses the term 'process model' and the DSDM Atern manual uses the term 'lifecycle', the terms in this case are synonymous. The combination of the two processes is initially done using diagrams. Then each PRINCE2 process is explored in detail.

7.1 REPRESENTATIONS OF EACH PROCESS

The PRINCE2 process model (Figure 7.1) has the eight management processes. It is arranged chronologically from left to right and maps onto the PRINCE2 management structure, where project direction is at the top, project management is in the middle and product delivery is at the bottom level.

Figure 7.2 shows the DSDM Atern lifecycle and is affectionately known as the 'cheese and pizzas' diagram. The cheese represents two sequential stages to ensure a sound understanding of the project before moving into the iterative development of the solution, which is deployed incrementally.

When combining the two methods the PRINCE2 process model can be left as it is and the pizzas and deployment can be taken from the DSDM Atern lifecycle to enable product delivery to be carried out in a more agile way.

Figure 7.1 The PRINCE2 process model

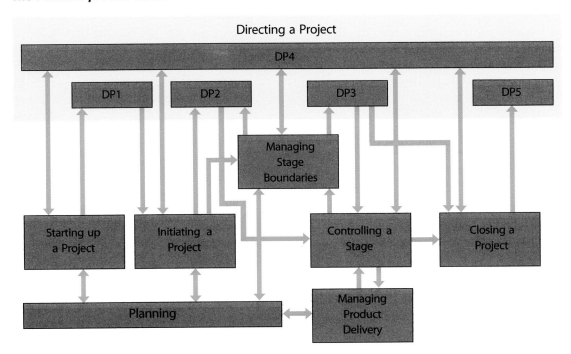

Figure 7.2 The DSDM Atern lifecycle

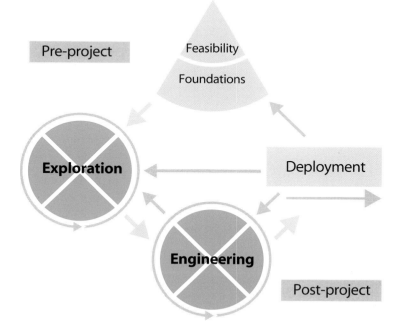

Figure 7.3 provides a linear representation of some of the PRINCE2 processes and the Project Board decision points. This is how it would be for a normal PRINCE2 project. Figure 7.3 shows three stages after DP2 (Authorising a Project) and it is inside these stages that DSDM Atern would be integrated.

When combining the two methods the contents of a stage can be shown in two ways. The most straightforward is illustrated in Figure 7.4, where a stage is shown to comprise several Work Packages. Figure 7.5 shows a stage broken down into three increments. In DSDM Atern an increment is a delivery of a product (or a partial delivery of a product) typically into operational use. However, it is not always possible to deliver a product into operational use, but the feedback from the incremental delivery is still highly desirable.

Increments are high-level timeboxes and increments can be used to help keep a PRINCE2 stage within its time tolerance.

The contents of a Work Package when integrating PRINCE2 and DSDM Atern can take several forms, but they will all comprise one or more timeboxes, which may or may not result in a deployment.

Therefore a Work Package could contain just one timebox (Figure 7.6a).

Or it could contain several timeboxes (Figure 7.6b).

Or it could contain timeboxes and a deployment (Figure 7.6c).

Figure 7.3 The Project Manager's perspective of the PRINCE2 processes

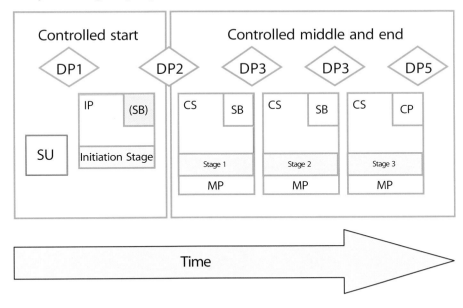

Figure 7.4 Work Packages within a management stage

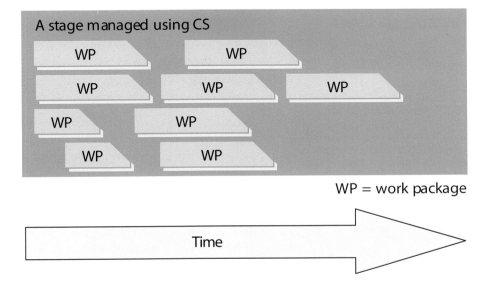

Figure 7.5 Work Packages within a management stage delivered incrementally

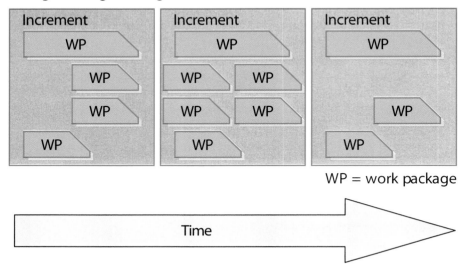

7.2 MAPPING DSDM ATERN TO PRINCE2 DURING THE CONTROLLED START

There are variations on how to map the DSDM Atern lifecycle onto PRINCE2. The most straightforward and the preferred option is to align them as shown in Table 7.1.

Table 7.1 Mapping the DSDM Atern lifecycle onto PRINCE2

PRINCE2	Atern phase	DSDM v4.2 phase
Project Mandate (A29)	Pre-project	Pre-project
Starting up a Project (SU)	Feasibility	Feasibility study
Initiating a Project (IP)	Foundations	Business study

When doing this there are two considerations that need to take place:

- The level of detail at which the Project Initiation Document (PID) should be maintained
- Which DSDM Atern products to use to complement the information in the PID.

To enable PRINCE2 to work in a more agile way there needs to more emphasis on understanding the fundamentals of the problem to be solved during the controlled start as opposed to actually solving them. This involves shifting the emphasis slightly from defining what the products are to what the products need to do.

This is achieved by adding supporting information to the PID, which explains more business and technical information about the objective of the project in order to gauge more accurately how long it will take and how much it will cost.

Figure 7.6 Examples of Work Package contents

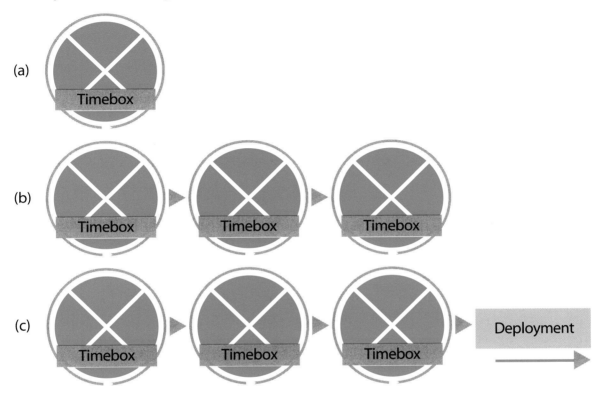

7.2.1 The PID

When integrating PRINCE2 with DSDM Atern the PID should be baselined at a high level of detail from the perspective of the products needed for a solution. This may be at a higher level of detail than on a PRINCE2-only project. The subsequent use of the DSDM Atern pizzas can then take this understanding (and the products needed) down a level as a clearer understanding of the detailed nature of the problem develops.

7.2.2 DSDM Atern products

To help complement the PID with information to enable a convergent approach to building a solution, it is recommended that the products listed in Table 7.2 are included. These can be incorporated into the PID or provided separately. It is not necessary to write Product Descriptions for them or treat them as specialist products.

7.2.3 Controlled start mapping – variations

There are variations which can be used in certain circumstances.

Smaller projects can merge the SU and IP processes and the equivalent DSDM Atern products accordingly where direction during the controlled start can be less formal.

Table 7.2 Description of DSDM Atern products

DSDM Atern product	Description	Guidance	DSDM v4.2
Business Foundations: Prioritised Requirements List (PRL)	A list of features required. This will evolve from a high level of understanding to a detailed one as the project progresses.	Essential	PRL
Business Foundations: Business Area Definition (BAD)	A description of the business 'as is' and/or 'to be'. This can be in any form, such as defining business processes or the business context.	Desirable	BAD
Solution Foundations: Solution Architecture Definition (SAD)	A description of the technical and architectural environment in which the final product will be produced and become operational.	Desirable	SAD
Feasibility and Management Foundations: Project Approach Questionnaire (PAQ)	An assessment of the strengths and weaknesses of the project environment from a people, process and technology perspective in order to understand the best way to execute the project.	Desirable	S/RL

Very complex projects may wish to carry on refining the two DSDM Atern products of the BAD and the SAD for a period after the PID has been approved. This can create an escape route if it transpires that assumptions made in the PID are not accurate enough to proceed without further direction from the Project Board. Therefore a short management stage comprising an extended foundation phase can take place.

A further option would be to run a separate PRINCE2 feasibility project if the complexity was such that several options needed to be assessed.

Another option would be to map the whole of the controlled start in PRINCE2 to the feasibility phase in DSDM Atern. This is sometimes referred to as 'PID lite', where a very high-level PID is created quickly with the Business Case and Project Plan in outline only. This approach has often been used by DSDM organisations which are starting to adopt PRINCE2 as well. Over time organisations stay with this concept or switch over to using the Project Brief instead, which is in line with the

preferred option originally mentioned at the beginning of this section.

7.3 ITERATIVE AND INCREMENTAL PRODUCT DEVELOPMENT

Work Packages are used as the vehicle to deliver the agile style of working in an iterative and incremental way. This is the mechanism that acts as the interface between Controlling a Stage (CS) and Managing Product Delivery (MP).

From within Managing Product Delivery, timeboxing will be used to ensure that the potential to over-elaborate or over-engineer when iterating is avoided. It will also support the principle of always being 'on time' and therefore keeping the stage and the project on schedule and to budget.

It is possible that a team or Project Manager may describe Authorising Work Package (CS1) as 'authorising a timebox'. The preferred description would be to refer to work given to team members or subcontractors as Work Packages (which contain one or more timeboxes) but the different descriptions are normally regarded as synonymous. It is also the case that Team Plan is synonymous with timebox or 'timebox plan'.

The formality of how a Work Package is handed over will depend on factors such as the type of customer–supplier relationship. The use of Work Packages can be dropped altogether and replaced by just sanctioning timeboxes if the informal lines of communication are very good. This would help the agile way of working, but is not a prerequisite.

7.3.1 Work Package types

A Work Package will use a timebox to deliver one or more products. These products may be products in their own right or sub-products. They may also be complete or partial deliveries, as part of a cycle of iterations.

As well as this, the product could be a DSDM Atern exploration product or a DSDM Atern engineering product. DSDM Atern uses iterative development to examine what needs to be built and then to build it. These two steps relate to the two DSDM Atern pizzas known as 'exploration' and 'engineering'.

A Work Package could contain either exploration products only or engineering products only or a mixture of both where the initial work of the Work Package would involve exploring the needs of the product before actually building it.

7.3.2 Horizontal and vertical iteration

When integrating PRINCE2 with DSDM Atern there are broadly speaking two ways of creating a Project or Stage Plan and this relates to sequencing of the Work Packages.

One approach is to create several exploration Work Packages and build up a broad understanding of the final product. This would be followed by several engineering Work Packages, which would then build the actual products. This is known as horizontal product development.

The opposite approach would be to select a product and create an exploration Work Package for it and then create an engineering Work Package immediately afterwards. This would enable early delivery of some of the products before the whole of the product is fully understood in detail. This leads to the benefits of incremental delivery as described in Chapter 5. This approach is known as vertical product development.

These two options are at opposite ends of a spectrum and therefore a blend of the two can be used as appropriate. Vertical product development is typically the more agile approach.

7.4 THE USE OF THE EIGHT PRINCE2 PROCESSES

The eight processes of PRINCE2 are scalable and should be tailored to the needs of the project. PRINCE2 advises that each process should be approached with the question 'How extensively should this process be used on this project?'

When integrating PRINCE2 with DSDM Atern some adjustments to the processes are necessary. Most adjustments to the PRINCE2 method are covered in Chapter 9.

Table 7.3 PRINCE2 processes

PRINCE2 process	ID	Guidance
Starting up a Project	SU	This equates to feasibility in DSDM Atern. SU should be used as it is now, but it would be desirable to include the DSDM Atern Project Approach Questionnaire.
Initiating a Project	IP	This equates to foundations in DSDM Atern. IP should be used as it is now, but it would be essential to include the DSDM Atern PRL and desirable to include the DSDM Atern BAD and SAD. It would also be desirable to evolve the information in the DSDM Atern Project Approach Questionnaire if it had been created previously in SU.
Controlling a Stage	CS	CS does not have an equivalent process in DSDM Atern so it should be used as it is now. CS is a process for the Project Manager who is responsible for the day-to-day management of the stage by handling Work Packages, risks and issues and reporting. As well as this the Project Manager manages the interfaces between the teams. The main factor to consider about CS when integrating PRINCE2 with DSDM Atern is how formal or informal these activities should be.
Managing Product Delivery	MP	This process allows the controlled break between project management and product delivery. When integrating PRINCE2 with DSDM Atern this is the process that enables PRINCE2 also to provide product delivery. Inside MP the DSDM Atern phases of exploration, engineering and deployment will operate. The formality of this 'control break' will depend on the characteristics of the project and can be very formal or very informal. Typically (although not necessarily always) MP will be executed in the form of a team working on a timebox. Therefore the Work Package received into MP will contain the relevant Product Description(s), which may be baselined at a high level or a detailed level, and a Team Plan in the form of a timebox plan.
Managing Stage Boundaries	SB	SB does not have an equivalent process in DSDM Atern so it should be used as it is now. DSDM Atern has the concept of an increment, which is a delivery of a set of features typically into operational use. This is not necessarily Business Case driven (although it can be) and is therefore not quite the same as SB. However, DSDM Atern increments are high-level timeboxes and can enable a stage to finish on time; they could appear as subdivisions of a stage, but they would not cross the stage boundary.

Table 7.3 PRINCE2 processes ... continued

PRINCE2 process	ID	Guidance
Closing a Project	CP	CP should be used as it is now, but it has a limitation in that a project integrating PRINCE2 with DSDM Atern will normally deliver incrementally and therefore a lot of information collected in CP will already exist. An example of this would be that some of the final product may already be operational and therefore operational and maintenance acceptance would exist and be in use. Another example is that business benefit may already be accruing. The reason why information would already be available is that DSDM Atern deployments would already have taken place. This information needs to be captured and this can be done by creating the relevant PRINCE2 management products (produced during CP) early on in the project. Alternatively, the DSDM Atern Project Review Report (not a PRINCE2 Management Product) could be used in the form of a holding area until the last stage of the project was nearing completion. Therefore CP will still remain at the end of the project as a whole, but it will be a smaller process and act as a process that will consolidate all the information collected so far. It will then ensure that nothing is left unfinished and that the Project Board is notified of the project end.
Planning	PL	PL should be used as it is now unless the plan to be created is for a low-level timebox. This would normally be handled differently. There is no specific planning technique or process in DSDM Atern, although there is guidance on how to build a plan for a timebox. PL could be used to build a timebox depending on the amount of dependencies in the timebox and how obvious they are. Where dependencies are reasonably obvious there is little benefit in using the whole of the PL process (e.g. product-based planning) to create a timebox. The Product Description step of product-based planning would still be used in most situations. Timeboxing can be used for any level of plan in PRINCE2. If timeboxing is only being used at team level then PL would operate as normal for creating Project and Stage Plans. It is common for a planner or Project Manager to use PL to create a plan. A timebox would normally be built collectively by the team.
Directing a Project	DP	There is no need to change DP. Although no changes are required to the process the level of formality will need to be decided during IP4 (Setting up Project Controls). Working in an agile way is as appropriate at Project Board level as it is anywhere else on the project.

8 The combined organisation structure

In terms of project roles, responsibilities and team structures PRINCE2 and DSDM Atern dovetail in a very simple and straightforward way. This is because PRINCE2 concentrates on creating a Project Management Team that is focused on giving the project direction and managing the project in accordance with that direction. The PRINCE2 Project Management Team does not cover project delivery other than to set up a communication line with the Team Managers responsible for delivering products.

In contrast to PRINCE2, DSDM Atern covers both project governance and delivery. When combining the two methods there is no need to use the governance roles in DSDM Atern because this is one of the strengths of PRINCE2.

Several DSDM Atern roles would be used to support project delivery. There are three DSDM Atern roles that can be used to synchronise with PRINCE2 in order to join to the two organisational structures together.

On any project within any organisation there can be a multitude of permutations for roles and responsibilities on a project. The combined Project Management and Delivery Team suggested in Figure 8.1 is the most straightforward and an ideal place to start from.

8.1 THE PRINCE2 PROJECT MANAGEMENT TEAM – GUIDANCE

Generally all of the PRINCE2 roles are unaffected when combining the two methods in terms of responsibilities, but the following points may be of interest.

The Project Board:

- Needs to be aware that the project is being managed in an agile way and therefore may need 'awareness' training
- Should be aware that even if the project does not slip the deadline or overspend, it does not mean all is well – too much descoping may be happening
- Must give a quick response when issues are escalated to Project Board level to avoid too much disruption to timeboxes at stage or team level.

The Project Manager:

- Should not copy the concept of 'management by exception' because the frequent delivery of products will be providing the most information on the status of a stage
- Should let the teams create timeboxes in order to get ownership
- Should be aware that Checkpoint Reports are primarily about products delivered and not about time or cost
- Is responsible for cross-team communication, particularly regarding features being delivered.

The Team Manager:

- Is responsible for getting the team to create timeboxes.

Project Assurance:

- Should assure the project with an agile perspective (for example should consider whether the eight principles of DSDM Atern are being respected)
- Is ideally provided by a Technical Coordinator and Business Visionary, which would link the two organisational structures, although this is not necessarily the case.

Figure 8.1 The combined organisational structure of PRINCE2 and DSDM Atern

PRINCE2/DSDM Atern Organisation

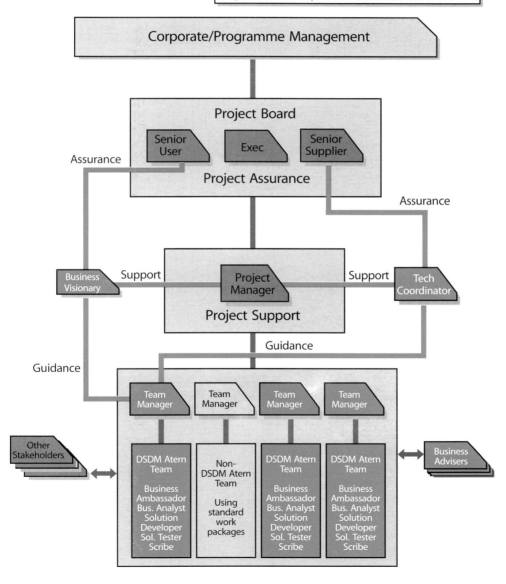

ɔject Support:

- Should be able to provide facilitation and scribing resources
- Would ideally provide DSDM Atern mentoring
- Needs to be aware of the different needs of an agile project.

8.2 DSDM ATERN ROLES

The combined organisational structure would introduce the following DSDM Atern roles.

8.2.1 Business Visionary

This is a senior business role. The Business Visionary is actively involved in interpreting the strategic needs of the Executive and Senior User to the teams. The Business Visionary is seen very much as someone who is championing the product being delivered by the project. This can possibly be a linking role between PRINCE2 and DSDM Atern and ideally this would take the PRINCE2 role of Project Assurance.

However, it is important that if the person carrying out this role does take on Project Assurance, that person should have a keen interest in the outcome of the project and be correctly delegated to/from the Executive and Senior User. Sometimes Project Assurance is independent not only of the Project Manager, but of the Project Board. This would be an implementation problem.

It is also possible that the person carrying out this role may sit on the Project Board.

8.2.2 Technical Coordinator

The Technical Coordinator ensures that the products being developed by the teams are technically sound and comply with the appropriate standards. This can also possibly be a linking role between PRINCE2 and DSDM Atern and ideally this would also take the PRINCE2 role of Project Assurance.

The Technical Coordinator performs the same function, from a technical perspective, as the Business Visionary does from a business perspective and would also need to have the same level of interest in the project outcome if carrying out the Project Assurance role.

8.2.3 Team Leader

The Team Leader is the third of the three linking roles and can be ignored if the use of the PRINCE2 Team Manager is preferred. They more or less cover the same function.

8.2.4 Business Ambassador

The Business Ambassador has a pivotal role when integrating PRINCE2 with DSDM Atern and enables an agile environment to exist within the team that is delivering the solution. The person with this business role provides the day-to-day communication channels between the project and the business. This is not necessarily a senior position, but it does need to be an empowered person who is chosen carefully to represent the business interests of those who will be impacted most by the delivery of the final product. It should not be confused with the PRINCE2 role of Senior User. The Business Ambassador helps with product delivery as opposed to giving project direction.

8.2.5 Business Adviser

Often a peer of the Business Ambassador, the Business Adviser provides complementary information, but with less involvement than the Business Ambassador. The Business Adviser acts as a 'sanity check' to the Business Ambassador and keeps other stakeholders affected by the project up to date.

8.2.6 Business Analyst

The Business Analyst sits within the product delivery team and focuses on the relationship between the business and technical roles in order to ensure that the business needs are properly analysed and are correctly described in the PRL and the Product Descriptions.

8.2.7 Solution Developer

The Solution Developer has a specialist role and must have the appropriate skills to be able to develop the products required. Ideally the Solution Developer is able to be business focused and customer facing as well as skilled in modelling and prototyping.

8.2.8 Solution Tester

DSDM Atern believes that one skill is needed to create or develop something and another to check that it is correct. Early versions of DSDM Atern did not have the role of Solution Tester, but feedback from DSDM Consortium members resulted in the creation of this role as part of best practice. A Solution Tester is able to advise the technical and business sides of the team, but may not be involved in the initial technical testing of a product.

This role overlaps with the role of Quality Checker or Reviewer in PRINCE2.

8.2.9 DSDM Atern Coach

DSDM Atern also believes that best practice involves the use of a method mentor – a DSDM Atern Coach – who can advise on the use of DSDM Atern or running a combination of PRINCE2 with DSDM Atern. This is not an administrative role and requires a lot of subject matter expertise to help the people on the project. The DSDM Atern Coach could sit quite happily as part of the team in Project Support or could operate independently as Project Assurance. The choice would depend on the skill level of

the team, in that an inexperienced team would need help, whereas an experienced team may merely need checking.

8.2.10 Other roles

The role of Business Sponsor is not required (use PRINCE2 Executive).

The role of Project Manager is not required (use PRINCE2 Project Manager).

9 The use of the PRINCE2 components

There are eight components which are used by the processes of PRINCE2 and this chapter gives guidance on when it is appropriate to adapt them when running PRINCE2 in combination with DSDM Atern (see Figure 2.1).

9.1 BUSINESS CASE

Both PRINCE2 and DSDM Atern emphasise the importance of the Business Case to the justification of a project. When integrating PRINCE2 with DSDM Atern the Business Case component in PRINCE2 requires a few minor adjustments to incorporate the needs of an agile project.

These minor adjustments result from using incremental delivery and managing the scope of the project. There may also be the need to include the fact that the project itself is integrating PRINCE2 with DSDM Atern.

The use of incremental delivery may mean that benefits are realised before the end of the project. These benefits may actually be funding later stages of the project and therefore this needs to be explained when describing the expected benefits. It is not uncommon that without incremental delivery the project is not viable.

The fact that scope is being actively managed on the project also needs to be documented in the Business Case because it may have a slight impact on the expected benefits. It must be stressed that this would typically be slight because anything more significant would represent a situation where too much of the project had not been delivered. A clear example of this would be a 'Should have' requirement being missed out.

A final adjustment that may be appropriate is to document the effect that integrating PRINCE2 with DSDM Atern may have on the project, particularly if this is not the regular method of product delivery. The choice of using this combination can be viewed as both positive and negative. On the one hand a combined approach can introduce more risk if it is in contrast to an organisation's existing culture. Alternatively, it could be the case that the only way to achieve a viable Business Case is to deliver the project in such a way.

One example of how integrating PRINCE2 with DSDM Atern could make the Business Case for a project is that the principle of delivering on time could cap the costs of a project, which are prone to escalate when a deadline is missed.

Specific changes to the PRINCE2 Business Case management product are described in Appendix A.

9.2 ORGANISATION

When integrating PRINCE2 with DSDM Atern it is necessary to expand the organisational structure outlined in the organisation component. PRINCE2 describes four layers of management and they should remain unchanged, but a fifth layer should be added to reflect the product delivery team.

There is no need to change the concept of there being three project interests (business, user and supplier) and that PRINCE2 is defined in terms of a customer who wants a product and a supplier who has the necessary skills to create that product.

The two organisational structures of PRINCE2 and DSDM Atern integrate easily. Perhaps the only difficulty in understanding this is that the three project interests mentioned before are not mentioned in the same way in each method.

This is because each approach has evolved from a different starting point from their origins as IT methods.

PRINCE2 is largely written from a customer's perspective whereas DSDM Atern is written from a supplier's perspective. Therefore DSDM Atern does reflect the three project interests defined by PRINCE2, but it does so by referring to the customer as 'the business focus'.

The integration of the two organisational structures from PRINCE2 and DSDM Atern is so fundamental to running PRINCE2 in a more agile way that it warrants a chapter specifically on this subject. This is covered in detail in Chapter 8.

9.3 PLANS

The plans component in PRINCE2 covers the two areas of plan levels and plan elements. Generally speaking both of these areas can be used as they are now when integrating PRINCE2 with DSDM Atern, but DSDM Atern will introduce an additional type of plan and this will be different in structure from a PRINCE2 plan.

The additional type of plan is a timebox plan, needed to support the DSDM Atern technique of timeboxing. This is covered in detail in Chapter 10.

The most appropriate course of action is to retain the existing plan levels of PRINCE2 and not to adapt the plans component other than to mention that any PRINCE2 plan could be a DSDM Atern timebox and that this would have a different structure.

One consideration worth mentioning is that a stage could be broken down into several increment timeboxes when using DSDM Atern.

However, this would largely depend on the terminology used on a specific project and it would particularly affect the term 'Team Plan'. When integrating PRINCE2 with DSDM Atern the Team Plan would normally be a Timebox Plan and therefore the name chosen should be the one most natural to the team or organisation. It would be advisable that only one term is used. The same natural law would apply the term 'Exception Plan' if this was being used to describe a Team Plan that will no longer achieve its objective or finish within tolerance.

9.4 CONTROLS

The controls component represents a large part of PRINCE2 because it is here that PRINCE2 describes each concept used to give PRINCE2 the mechanisms to enable project governance. These concepts can take many forms such as a management product, a process, a sub-process, a component or a technique.

There is no need to change the underlying concept of the PRINCE2 process model being event driven or the use of management stages.

When integrating PRINCE2 with DSDM Atern, many of the controls can remain unchanged because this is where PRINCE2 is very strong, but some will need to be adapted and new controls added.

One important decision to make at the outset is about the degree of control. A more agile way of working would involve a softer line at team level where an empowered team is actively managing scope from within a timebox. An example of this is the detail to which a Product Description is baselined. Working in an agile way would typically prefer the baseline to be higher than in a more traditional environment.

Another example of being agile is the use of informal communication lines, which can prove to be faster and more accurate than traditional document-driven approaches. Although this may appear counter-intuitive, it results in a greater level of control. However, there is an element of risk involved with this and it needs to be correctly managed.

When running PRINCE2 and DSDM Atern in combination it is generally preferable to use more informal methods of control within the empowered teams and more formal methods outside the team. This is in keeping with PRINCE2 focusing on project management and DSDM Atern focusing on product delivery.

9.4.1 Project Board controls

Project Board controls would remain largely as they are, but they would need to include information specifically about scope in order to ascertain if the project should continue or not. This applies from Authorising Initiation (DP1) to Confirming Project Closure (DP5).

One particular Project Board control to adjust is the Highlight Report, which needs to inform the Project Board accurately how the scope of the project is being managed. When using PRINCE2 with DSDM Atern it is possible to set an immovable deadline and a fixed budget. Timeboxing will then act as the control to hit the deadline with no cost overrun. When doing this it is important that the Project Board understands what to look at in order to ensure that the project is under control.

To put this in another way, if the Project Board is only looking at budget and schedule status it will have no idea of the stage status because it is expected to be on time and on cost. The more important question concerns the amount of scope of the project that is being delivered. This could be handled by using 'Products completed during the period' but a tighter way would be to use the Highlight Report as described in Appendix A and use 'Scope status'.

What the Project Board should be looking for is the speed of product delivery. This is sometimes referred to as velocity and can provide an early check on the accuracy of estimates.

9.4.2 Project start-up

The primary adjustment to be considered to the controlled start of a project using PRINCE2 and DSDM Atern concerns the level of detail of the Project Initiation Document (PID). An agile way of working would prefer a PID that has been baselined at a high level. That is not to say that this baselining should be at too high a level because this would not be in keeping with the correct application of PRINCE2.

The level of detail in the PID is covered in more detail in Chapter 7.

Another adjustment to make at this point would be to document in the Communication Plan how everyone on the project is going to communicate. This provides the opportunity to decide specifically what is to be informal (to enable agility) and what is not.

The most important single control in PRINCE2 is the concept of using management stages. When integrating PRINCE2 with DSDM Atern these stages may contain one or more increments, which could help to ensure that each stage finishes on time and within budget. This could be planned for during the project start-up or delayed until planning the next stage.

9.4.3 Controlled progress

Most of the controls in PRINCE2 are concentrated on this part of the project and with one particular exception they should remain largely unchanged, although a few minor adjustments are still needed.

The exception refers to the use of tolerance as a control. PRINCE2 is built around the two standard elements of tolerance: time and cost. When running PRINCE2 and DSDM Atern together, the status of scope as a tolerance needs to be elevated to the same level as time and cost if not higher.

Management by exception should continue as it would normally, but the event that will trigger an Exception Report would typically be a timebox failing due to problems with the amount of scope being delivered.

Most of the controls used in controlled progress are PRINCE2 management products and guidance on these is given in Appendix A.

There are two other controls, namely the End Stage Assessment and the Exception Assessment (DP3 – Authorising a Stage or Exception Plan). They do not require any changes, but they could benefit from additional information collected regarding any business benefits which are being accrued through the use of incremental delivery.

These assessments may also benefit from being run by a facilitator.

9.4.4 Controlled close

A lot of information is generated at the end of a project for the Project Board. This enables the Project Board to confirm that the project has been completed and the Board can therefore close it. When integrating PRINCE2 with DSDM Atern, product delivery will be incremental, so this will need to be handled differently. The measures that need to be taken are described in Chapter 7.

9.4.5 Control in DSDM Atern

DSDM Atern is similar to PRINCE2 in many of the controls it has and when combining the two methods DSDM Atern will be primarily responsible for controlling Product Delivery. It does this with the use of timeboxing and MoSCoW. These two techniques work in tandem and can also be applied equally well at stage level and project level.

Specific changes to each of the 36 management products are described in Appendix A.

9.5 MANAGEMENT OF RISK

This component remains largely unchanged when integrating PRINCE2 with DSDM Atern. It only requires some minor adjustments and additional guidance on how to handle the DSDM Atern approach to risk.

9.5.1 Risk management cycle

The most significant part of this component is the risk management cycle and this needs a minor adjustment. The selection step of risk analysis focuses on balancing the cost of the control action in relation to the risk. Although this could remain as it is, it would be more appropriate in an agile environment to view it from the perspective of value lost and not cost. This would enable the impact of the risk to be assessed from the viewpoint of scope, thereby allowing a decision to be made based on the effect of reducing the scope on the final product. To put this in another way, it would be typical for the impact of a risk where DSDM Atern is handling the product delivery to have no effect at all on the cost of the project.

9.5.2 Uncovering risk in DSDM Atern

Although there would be no need to change the management of risk component it is important to understand that when integrating PRINCE2 with DSDM Atern, the DSDM Atern approach uses two specific practices that aim to uncover risks.

The first is the early Project Approach Questionnaire, which examines the approach being taken on the project and any risks inherent with that approach. An example of this is where one project is taking place across different continents and another is taking place at just one site. The Project Approach Questionnaire would highlight the risks involved with communication on the first project, which would not be as significant on the second.

Also included in this assessment is an analysis of the primary area of concern when using DSDM Atern. This relates to the ability of the project to adhere to the eight principles of DSDM Atern. Any compromise here would detrimentally affect the ability of the project to be classed as agile. This can take place as part of SU5 – Defining Project Approach.

The second practice is that of daily meetings or 'wash-ups', which include a question on potential problems. Therefore the product delivery team may capture risks every day and the Project Manager may wish to be involved in this or at least be aware of the output. Sometimes mini-Risk Logs are held for the life of a timebox.

9.5.3 External risks

In terms of risk management, PRINCE2 does not differentiate between risks that are internal to the team and external risks over which the team has much less control. However, when integrating PRINCE2 with DSDM Atern it may be appropriate to be less tolerant of external risks because of the need of DSDM Atern to be on time. An example of this is where a third party is supplying something and it may arrive late. A product delivery team has a lot of control over ensuring internal deliveries are punctual, but the same cannot be said of products which are external to the team or the project as a whole.

9.6 QUALITY IN A PROJECT ENVIRONMENT

The component most affected by integrating PRINCE2 with DSDM Atern is that of quality in a project environment. Both methods place a very strong emphasis on the importance of this area, but they do so with different styles, which are contrasting rather than complementary. The contrast does not represent a problem when integrating PRINCE2 with DSDM Atern, but it is necessary to understand the implications of the adjustments needed.

The fundamental difference in style is inherited from the basic ethos of each method, where PRINCE2 tends to be more predictive and DSDM Atern is more convergent. Particularly in the area of Product Descriptions, PRINCE2 strives for things to be accurate, complete and unambiguous from the outset, whereas DSDM Atern prefers to baseline understanding in order to converge on accuracy later on. This affects how the quality path in this component is implemented.

Another effect on the quality path comes from the attitude towards change, which is different in both methods. The quality path needs to be implemented in such a way that change can be easily accommodated and not be the root cause of product failures.

An example of this is the need to understand the reality of a situation whereby dropping a couple of low-priority features from a product could result in a well built product being delivered on time and thereby maximising a business opportunity. This should not be regarded in any way as a quality failure, despite the fact that part of the product has not been delivered. This can happen where the implementation of a quality policy or quality system has been overzealous.

9.6.1 Additional quality system processes

When integrating PRINCE2 with DSDM Atern there are additional checks to be made by quality assurance or project assurance to ensure that the approach to product delivery is being carried out correctly.

Specific checks would include:

- Is the business involvement in the project being maintained?
- Are timeboxes being respected?
- Are facilitated workshops being used appropriately?
- Is the appropriate amount of reviewing taking place?

Further to this the contrasts mentioned earlier need to be inspected to ensure that the use of a convergent approach or the acceptance of dynamic change is being correctly applied and that neither is in itself causing a degradation of the level of quality.

Several management products are involved in the quality path. Guidance for each one is provided as part of Appendix A.

If PRINCE2 is part of an existing corporate or programme quality system it would be appropriate to add the combined approach of running PRINCE2 with DSDM Atern to it as well.

9.7 CONFIGURATION MANAGEMENT

The Configuration Management component is in a similar position to the previous component of quality in a project environment in that PRINCE2 and DSDM Atern both see this as vitally important, but they approach it from contrasting directions. Again, the reason for this comes from the differing needs of a predictive approach as opposed to a convergent one.

There is little to change with this component when integrating PRINCE2 with DSDM Atern, but there is the need for additional guidance to explain the different needs of each method. The fundamental reason for the different needs is that DSDM Atern is an iterative method and PRINCE2 is not explicitly iterative.

Configuration Management in PRINCE2 is closely linked to the product-based planning technique where all products are identified and described. The purpose of Configuration Management in PRINCE2 is to identify, track and protect the projects products. A more agile way of working would focus more on the tracking aspect than protection.

When integrating PRINCE2 with DSDM Atern there is no need to decouple the close link between product-based planning and Configuration Management because both methods are based on a product focus as opposed to an activity focus. However, there are choices to be made after the products have been identified.

A decision must be taken about what to configuration manage when in an agile environment. It may be appropriate to leave certain low-level sub-products out because managing them would not be of any benefit, or it may be that they are still relatively undefined and would be so volatile that they would represent an unnecessary overhead.

When developing a product iteratively, Configuration Management is needed in order to keep the product and any supporting products in line. The ability to reverse is important when developing iteratively, but this can be hampered if certain elements to help build a product have (perhaps erroneously) been left outside Configuration Management and may therefore not be in line. An example of this is where testing documentation and test data are not consistent with the version of the product being checked.

It is important use Configuration Management correctly right from the outset of a project when integrating PRINCE2 with DSDM Atern. This affects the day-to-day running of the project as well as the long-term view, because the DSDM Atern approach uses an iterative and incremental approach to developing products in order to converge on an accurate solution.

Iteration is a concept that could take place several times in one day or over several weeks or months. Similarly, the concept of incremental delivery can take place over many months, but may also occur weekly where partial deliveries of the overall solution can be accommodated. There are cases where incremental delivery can take place daily.

This enforces the need for Configuration Management to be applied at the right level and with the appropriate level of rigour. Too much Configuration Management will slow down a project and too little could also slow it down as time is taken to rectify mistakes.

9.8 CHANGE CONTROL

This is the last of the eight components of PRINCE2 and it is closely linked to the previous component of Configuration Management. It could be argued that Change Control and Configuration Management are also very closely related to the broad philosophy of quality in

PRINCE2 (and therefore the component of quality in a project environment).

It is therefore no coincidence that this component is also affected by the contrasting approaches of PRINCE2 and DSDM Atern. Perhaps this component is the one where the contrast is at its greatest. The language that each method uses to refer to change is very different. PRINCE2 refers to it in a more negative way than DSDM Atern and this is a key differentiator between an agile approach and one that is not.

However, this is not to say that PRINCE2 cannot be agile and when integrating PRINCE2 with DSDM Atern this can be addressed. Although there are differences in this area there are also significant similarities. Both approaches use a controlled start in order to ascertain a solid understanding of the needs of the project. Both approaches also accept the inevitability of change. However, there are significant changes needed to the Change Control component when running PRINCE2 and DSDM Atern together.

9.8.1 The level of formality

First, Project Issue management will operate in two ways. The first way is as described in the Change Control component whereby Project Issues are formally captured, logged, categorised and their impact assessed. This will be used for significant issues that an empowered team delivering product cannot solve on its own.

The second way Project Issue management will operate is very informally whereby the empowered team can raise and address Project Issues very quickly by leveraging the agile way of working.

It is possible that this component can be used unchanged. This would be achieved by the Project Manager allowing the Team Manager to manage Project Issues within the product delivery team in a very informal way, but anything outside the team would be handled formally. However,

when integrating PRINCE2 with DSDM Atern in order to create an agile approach to project management, there needs to a higher level of baselining when describing products so that changes to the low-level detail of them will not trigger the formal mechanics of Change Control unnecessarily. This is sometimes described as setting the breadth of the scope, but not the depth of the scope.

It is perfectly acceptable in an agile environment to alter the detail of a product without going through Change Control. This can be achieved because the broader (higher level) description of the product has not changed. The integrity of the change is protected because the change will be made by the empowered team whose members are best positioned to understand the impact of the change.

This can feel counter intuitive, but embracing change is a key feature of the agile way of working and the benefit of this approach is speed of handling a change and the greater accuracy of the products being delivered.

9.8.2 The impact on scope

The most significant difference between handling issues in a predictive environment as opposed to a convergent one is to do with the impact of the change.

The Change Control component focuses on the impact of the change against the quality of a product, the project costs and the project timescales. On an agile project this can all be protected by making an adjustment to the project scope instead and as already mentioned this can be done very quickly.

Therefore the Change Control component needs to reflect that there is an alternative way of handling the impact of a change.

The mechanisms to enable this to happen such as business involvement, empowered teams, timeboxing and MoSCoW, are explained further in Chapter 10.

10 The use of PRINCE2 and DSDM Atern techniques

This chapter describes how to use each of the techniques covered by PRINCE2 and DSDM Atern when running both methods together. The advantages and benefits of using each technique were described in Chapters 4, 5 and 6. Refer to the PRINCE2 manual and the DSDM Atern manual for a complete description of each technique. The five techniques included with DSDM Atern are there because they are regarded as best practice and many users of PRINCE2 may already be using some or all of them.

DSDM Atern has five techniques which give PRINCE2 a product delivery capability. PRINCE2 has three techniques, none of which are mandated, but it would be difficult to imagine running a PRINCE2 project without using product-based planning. Specific techniques are outside the scope of PRINCE2.

10.1 TIMEBOXING (DSDM ATERN)

Timeboxing fits in easily to PRINCE2 because PRINCE2 and DSDM Atern both see planning as having three levels. There are several ways to implement timeboxing when integrating PRINCE2 with DSDM Atern and this is dictated by the choice of what to timebox and at what level.

10.1.1 Levels of timeboxing

There are three levels at which timeboxing can be used with PRINCE2, which correspond to the three plan levels of project, stage and team. Depending on the needs of the project it may be appropriate to only use timeboxing at team level where a timebox is agreed with a team as it is handed over in a Work Package. However, this would mean that only the product delivery was taking place in an agile way and that project governance was not.

The more timeboxing is used with the higher levels of PRINCE2 plan the more agile the project becomes. Therefore a project can be timeboxed and so can a stage. When integrating PRINCE2 with DSDM Atern it would be normal to timebox at all three levels because control is best achieved when the three levels are connected. The effect of connecting as many levels as possible is that this gives a high degree of control. If a low-level timebox (e.g. at Team Plan level) fails then any connected timebox higher up in the hierarchy is also failing. Not only is this visible to the Project Manager or Project Board, but it is also visible very quickly.

There is one further consideration for timeboxing at stage level. An advantage of timeboxing a stage is that it enables on-time delivery of the stage and the checking of a projects ongoing viability. The control of this can be improved by breaking each management stage down into smaller increment timeboxes (Figure 10.1). This may result in operational products being delivered earlier and providing the end stage assessment with better information on which to judge project viability.

10.1.2 Timebox content

Timeboxes can be built in various ways, but all will be driven by the outputs from product-based planning. The choice depends on what content is most appropriate for a timebox and how iteration will be handled.

There are two decisions to take:

- Should the timebox comprise a single product or several products (multi-product)?
- Should iterations be contained within a timebox or should a timebox be created for each iteration?

Figure 10.1 How timeboxing levels can work with PRINCE2

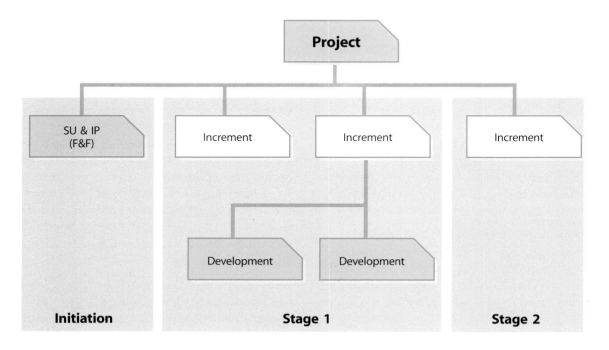

The decision on whether or not to use a multi-product timebox depends on how easy it would be to deliver the products as a set. DSDM Atern advocates the use of three iterations within a timebox (called investigation, refinement and consolidation) and a multi-product timebox would need all products moving through the timebox at a similar speed in order to do this.

How to represent iterations would be dictated by the Work Package mechanism and the normal approach would be to keep the iterations within the timebox.

10.1.3 Requirements-based planning

Product-based planning can be adapted to use requirements instead of products. There is little difference

in reality as a requirement can be treated in the same way as a product. The difference is that a product is more of a solution and a requirement is more of a problem or need. This is where the agile mindset of 'I'll know it when I see it' is different from the 'clearly and unambiguously defined' products of PRINCE2. The two views can live in harmony because they represent the same idea, but from a different angle or point in time. It is common practice on a DSDM Atern project to build a timebox with only requirements.

10.1.4 Tolerance

In a timebox there is no such concept as adding in time as a tolerance. The whole point of a timebox is that there is no time tolerance. The only tolerance available to the timebox team is that of scope. If the team is falling behind it has to reduce the content of the timebox.

10.2 FACILITATED WORKSHOPS (DSDM ATERN)

Facilitated workshops are a very powerful tool to use when integrating PRINCE2 with DSDM Atern, but they must be used appropriately to avoid excess. The first area where facilitated workshops can be introduced is to help shift the method of communication away from documentation to a more inter-personal one. This would mean creating the bulk of a document (such as a Project Quality Plan, a BAD, a SAD or a Communication Plan) in a workshop environment and reviewing it that way too. This is as opposed to one individual creating a document and circulating it for approval.

Early use of facilitated workshops can result in a project getting started very quickly and with outputs that are of a very high quality in that they are accurate and they have buy-in from the stakeholders. This is particularly useful because it is often the case that a project has been waiting for authorisation for a while and facilitated workshops can bring all of this together very quickly and enable decisions to be made. Two typical workshops held early in a project are a project launch workshop and a requirements gathering workshop involving MoSCoW.

Although facilitated workshops are commonly seen at the beginning of a project in order to help launch it, it is important to realise that they can be used throughout the project and they can be run in a variety of modes. Workshop examples include:

- Problem solving – where a technical or personnel problem looks like having a major impact on the project
- Planning – where groups can build plans together which result in high levels of speed and ownership

- Quality reviews – where the quality review technique in PRINCE2 can provide the structure of the workshop and guidance on who should attend
- Project and stage end reviews – where documents such as the Lessons Learned Report, End Project Report and End Stage Report can be created to describe what went well and what needs to be improved next time
- General reviewing – to ascertain feedback on such things as prototypes and models
- Design workshops – to harness the creativity of group working.

The use of facilitation can also breed a style of facilitative project management which can be a preferred way of managing for many people.

10.3 ITERATIVE DEVELOPMENT AND PROTOTYPING (DSDM ATERN)

Iterative development is often referred to as prototyping. This technique is used to increase understanding and communication on a project by creating one or more proofs of concept. This can be done at anytime on the project. Prototyping used early on in the project can be used to gain a clearer understanding of what the project is trying to produce. It can be used throughout a project to validate understanding or to help with the design of the product.

The use of prototyping helps with the convergent approach to building a product and can sometimes result in building another product before starting to build the final product. Prototyping can be used to fill in the detail of a Product Description which has been baselined before going in to the detail.

If prototyping is done during the controlled start of a project it can be perceived as not fitting in with the PRINCE2 process model because delivering product (albeit of limited functionality) only takes place in Managing

Product Delivery (MP) after the PID has been approved. When integrating PRINCE2 with DSDM Atern it is acceptable to issue Work Packages and use the MP process before leaving the controlled start in order to support prototyping.

Two examples of this are a very early disposable prototype to check the feasibility of a possible solution and a prototype to gain further understanding of a problem before going into 'solutioneering' (or problem-solving) mode.

10.4 MODELLING (DSDM ATERN)

There are many similarities between modelling and prototyping in the way they are used when integrating PRINCE2 with DSDM Atern. Their similarities can lead to an overlap whereby there can be confusion over whether or not something is a prototype or a model. As a general rule it is a model if it is static (such as a diagram) and it is a prototype if it is dynamic (such as a working mock-up). However, this is not always the case and the distinction is not really important because both techniques have the same goals in mind.

Modelling is also something that can be used throughout a project to aid understanding and communication. It is the visualisation and abstraction of a model which helps this happen. An example of a very common model is that of a process flowchart, which has a very simple syntax and is easily understood.

Extensive use of high-level models during the controlled start of a project is highly desirable when working in an agile way. This would take place in a way that supported the concept of convergence as models would evolve from a high level of understanding to a detailed understanding later in the project.

Unlike prototypes, modelling would not normally require the use of specialist skills and therefore would be

produced as a matter of course and not require the use of Work Packages.

10.5 MOSCOW PRIORITISATION (DSDM ATERN)

The MoSCoW technique is a simple one to learn, but there are specific considerations that need to be taken into account when using it on a project integrating PRINCE2 with DSDM Atern. The most important considerations are that this technique is used to help with the control of a project and it is used in conjunction with timeboxing and business involvement. The MoSCoWed feature list resides in the Prioritised Requirements List (PRL), a DSDM Atern product, which is added to the existing PRINCE2 management products.

The evolution of the PRL will be in line with the 'UTH rule' mentioned in Chapter 5. In the early stages of a project the understanding of the project's requirements will typically be at a high level and this may result in all of them being prioritised as a 'Must'. The ability to control a project through managing its scope will happen as the requirements are broken down into lower levels and there is the appropriate level of granularity to enable features to be dropped, changed or added.

Using MoSCoW to prioritise is reasonably straightforward when done individually, but when groups of stakeholders come together from different areas or from different levels of an organisation it can be difficult to get consensus. This is where facilitated workshops are valuable so that someone who is impartial can manage the process and it can be given the appropriate amount of time to take place because joining a MoSCoW list together can be time consuming.

When integrating PRINCE2 with DSDM Atern the general concept of MoSCoW is normally adopted throughout the project and can be used on such things as the Issue Log or an agenda.

10.6 PRODUCT-BASED PLANNING (PRINCE2)

This technique works well when integrating PRINCE2 with DSDM Atern because both methods focus on products as a means to define what needs to be created and how to monitor progress on a project.

The best way to use product-based planning when integrating PRINCE2 with DSDM Atern is to synchronise the evolving plans with that of the Prioritised Requirements List (PRL), which will also be evolving. In this way the contrasting views of what is required and what needs to be produced can be woven together.

This helps with baselining the Product Descriptions at the appropriate level. Therefore if a requirement is known in complete detail a Product Description can be written with a set of quality criteria that can ensure a product will meet its stated purpose. Alternatively, if a requirement is only understood in broad terms then any Product Descriptions associated with it can only be created in what PRINCE2 describes as a skeleton format.

Iteration can be shown in two ways when using product-based planning. The typical way to represent a product undergoing the normal three iterations would be to use one product, and information pertaining to the use of iteration would be contained in the appropriate Work Package.

An alternative way to represent this would be for each iteration to be a distinct product and then group them under a collective grouping. Integration products and simple products would operate in the normal way.

MoSCoW can be used on Product Descriptions, but this needs to handled carefully so as not to dilute one of the strongest controls (particularly of quality) in PRINCE2. An example of this is where quality criteria are defined in such a way that a product must be able to carry six passengers and should be able to carry seven passengers.

The danger with this is that it can lead to the essence of quality criteria being misapplied.

Although the PRINCE2 process model does not explicitly support iteration there are already structures within PRINCE2 that can change that perception. Product-based planning is one of them because it builds plans iteratively in response to the greater understanding of an evolving solution. It is an explicitly iterative technique and although this only applies within the remit of planning in PRINCE2 it can be used as the foundations to enable PRINCE2 to run in a more agile way.

10.7 QUALITY REVIEW TECHNIQUE (PRINCE2)

The quality review technique is optional in PRINCE2 and when integrating PRINCE2 with DSDM Atern this can be left to be used as it normally would be or it can be enhanced by combining it with the much wider remit of the facilitated workshop. There is a close alignment between the two and each has its own strengths. The quality review technique is in effect a workshop for one specific type of event and PRINCE2 provides good guidance on the preparation, review and follow-up needed for quality reviewing a product. This also covers the roles involved such as Project Assurance and the Configuration Librarian.

The Review Chairperson is similar to the Workshop Facilitator, but DSDM Atern sees a facilitator as having key skills at setting up and running these sorts of events. It is a role that is placed significantly higher than chairing, and a facilitator would come with several techniques and skills to run a quality review in the best way possible. These skills would cover the process of the quality review as well as the group dynamics of the individuals involved.

One particular area where the training of a facilitator may improve a quality review is in stopping a situation where the feedback on any limitations of a product is perceived as a criticism of the individual who produced it. It is common for the creator of a product to defend their work because they are closely attached to it. The aim of a quality review is to review the product not the person who created it and this is where the facilitator can help.

10.8 CHANGE CONTROL TECHNIQUE (PRINCE2)

This technique is optional in PRINCE2 and its use is covered in section 9.8.

Part 3
Example and conclusion

3

11 Simple scenario

This chapter provides an example of how DSDM Atern could work on a project which is integrating PRINCE2 and DSDM Atern. The example is deliberately a very simple one and is told in the form of a story. It concentrates on creating one specialist product in order to illustrate what events could take place when using DSDM Atern, who would be involved and when this would take place. The explanation of the way in which DSDM Atern works (in conjunction with PRINCE2 or not) is covered elsewhere in this publication. More detailed analysis of why DSDM Atern works can be found in other DSDM Atern publications.

This worked example will cover the additional benefits derived from using DSDM Atern with PRINCE2. It looks at the agile way of addressing a problem in that it deliberately tries to explore the problem before defining the solution by way of a specialist Product Description. It converges on what the Product Description should be and in some cases would let the Product Description emerge.

The example also tries to illustrate how iteration and incremental delivery would hit a deadline while being controlled by the use of the MoSCoW technique.

11.1 THE SCENARIO

The example chosen is based around the simple scenario given in the chapter on product-based planning in the PRINCE2 manual, which describes a project to organise and run a conference for between 75 and 90 delegates. There is no need to have this to hand, but it may help when trying to view this simple example in a wider context as the manual contains a Product Breakdown Structure, an example Product Description and a Product Flow Diagram.

The example in the PRINCE2 manual describes the conference as having a theme and is aimed at a particular profession. The conference is held at a venue, where a programme of speakers will be invited to present and there will be a handout pack for delegates. Bookings need to be handled, a press release needs to be issued and staff will need to be recruited for the event.

For the purposes of this publication it is assumed that the conference is being set up by a financial services training company. The conference will be aimed at bringing financial services professionals up to date with a new set of financial regulations and is entitled 'Saving for a rainy day'. It is hoped that the exposure the training company will get will lead to an increase in business. The overall final product will be the conference. This worked example will concentrate on creating a sub-product, which has been identified as the delegate handout pack.

It must be stressed that this is one way of going about creating a delegate handout pack and not the only way. It may well be the case that defining what is needed for the delegate handout pack is quite straightforward and a Product Description could be written immediately. This example will look at a situation where there are assumed to be many unknowns.

As soon as the need for a delegate handout pack has been identified and the Project Board has given authorisation to the plan containing it, a Work Package could be issued to create it.

When DSDM Atern is used for product delivery, the story may unfold as described next.

Background

The project team as a whole has never produced a delegate handout pack before and is unsure of the best way to go. The Project Board has approved the creation of one and the Project Manager is responsible for making sure this happens.

The Project Manager (called Chris) decides to issue a Work Package for the creation of the delegate handout pack to an internal team of four people led by a Team Manager. The Work Package is handled very informally and the Product Description contains only the title ('delegate handout pack') and its purpose is described as 'not sure really'. One other piece of information is that the Project Manager and the Team Manager have agreed that this Work Package involves a 10-day timebox.

The team comprises:

■ Sanjay, who is in charge of the training department and is the Team Leader

■ Mary from the training department as Business Ambassador

■ Adrian from courseware production as the Solution Developer and Solution Tester

■ Linda, who is a trainer and is the Business Analyst.

The team has two weeks to complete its objective. Their timebox starts on Monday of the first week and will last 10

working days. They are referred to in DSDM Atern as the Solution Development Team, but in this scenario they will be referred to as the timebox team.

Day 1 – Investigation

On Monday morning the timebox team and Chris come together to kick off the timebox by planning the next two weeks. Their first task is to clarify the objective of the timebox. They decide that the objective is to 'create a complete mock-up of the delegate handout pack'. The quality criteria for this could be that it could be physically handed over to someone for production (of 100 packs).

In DSDM Atern a low-level timebox is made up of three cycles called investigate, refine and consolidate. The timebox team opts for a 20%:60%:20% split and plans their work accordingly (see Figure 11.1).

The members of the team plan to run a facilitated workshop on Monday afternoon of the first week to find out what the requirements are for the delegate handout pack. They have arranged for the Senior User on the Project Board to attend this as they feel it will help position the workshop and give it clear direction about the output required.

Figure 11.1 The investigation–refinement–consolidation timebox

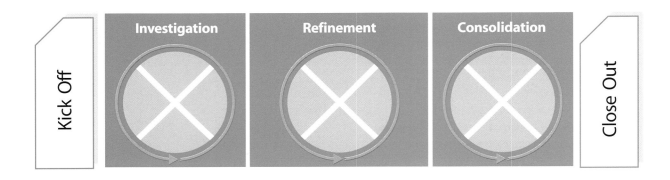

Table 11.1 Desired results for scenario after the investigation, refinement and consolidation cycles of the timebox

At the end of the:	Objective
Investigation cycle	To have a very rough concept at the end of Day 2, perhaps only drawings on flipchart paper, of what the delegate handout pack would be like.
Refinement cycle	To have a complete mock-up of what a delegate would be given at the conference. It may be held together with paperclips or tape, and graphics would be hand-drawn, but it will be the same size and have the same contents as the real thing.
Consolidation cycle	To have the final version ready to hand to production. This will involve deciding on what is in and what is out of the delegate handout pack.

The team has planned that each cycle of the timebox will produce the results shown in Table 11.1.

The team members would like to define a Product Description for the delegate handout pack, but cannot do this because they are currently unsure of what exactly they are trying to achieve with it. Therefore, if they can get a good understanding of what the delegate handout pack is supposed to do, they can then go about working out how to do it.

DSDM Atern uses the exploration pizza to address this. The exploration pizza is used to find out what it is that the business wants. This is used to determine the requirements and identify the features needed.

Later on, and not as part of this timebox, the engineering pizza is used to find out 'Is this it?' This is achieved by building the product and validating that it is correct.

The workshop proved very successful as lots of ideas were discussed such as the quality, the format and the logistics. These were then MoSCoWed and a Prioritised Requirements List (PRL) was produced (Table 11.2).

The team members were pleased with the list and the Senior User was able to say that having seen the list and bearing in mind that the conference was a prestigious event there was no restriction on budget. Therefore,

whatever could be sorted out by the end of next week could be included. The team was also clear that certain things were 'Musts', such as having a gift, but there were several options available and they were not all 'Musts' below this top level. This was going to help them hit the deadline.

It was also apparent that they may go with just one memory/USB stick (which would be the gift) and have everything on it and therefore no need for a bag. They would decide this at the end of Tuesday of the first week.

Day 2

The team is still in the early days of this exploration timebox and acutely aware of the fact that they are not exactly sure how they are going to do this, but they do know exactly what they have to produce. They also know that they have got to do it by the Friday of the second week and the only way they can guarantee hitting this deadline is by managing the content of the timebox.

They do not want to call on extra people to help because no one else was at the first workshop and therefore this would slow them down. Compromising on the quality of the delegate handout pack would not look good bearing in mind the nature of the event.

Table 11.2 Prioritised Requirements List for scenario after MoSCoW analysis

No.	Idea/Requirement	Priority	Notes
1	Include a gift:	M	
	• A book	C	May be heavy
	• A coaster	S	
	• A fluffy toy (8 inches)	C	Is popular and has logo on it
	• A plant	C	Small bonsai tree
2	Some form of case:	S	
	• With a strap	S	
	• Securely closable	C	Zip or simple toggles
	• Usable as a laptop bag	S	
	• Space for sponsorship on it	M	Will be seen by people
3	Use a memory/USB stick only	C	No need for a 'physical' pack
4	Pen	M	To write with at the conference
	Pencil	S	
5	Umbrella	S	Small one (on message with the conference)
6	Sun cream	C	Humorous idea?
7	Agenda on a postcard	C	For ease of reference
8	Feedback form	C	May do this by e-mail
9	Safety Instructions	M	Conference centre requires this by law
10	Presentations	S	Could refer delegates to the website

At the end of the first Tuesday team members came together and presented various options to the Senior User and selected Business Advisers to see what people's feelings were.

The overwhelming feedback was to go with a small case, if possible with a strap, and put into the pack the umbrella, the toy and a book. The pen and the safety instructions had to go in (they are 'Musts') and as the days progressed decisions could be made on the presentations, the agenda and the feedback form. This would be handled by the timebox team, whose members were empowered to decide this.

Day 3 – Refinement

The team then agreed on a plan on how to work with their new priorities over the next six days, which would lead up to the review at the end of the refinement cycle.

Chris was being kept informed by Sanjay every two days with a Checkpoint Report via e-mail. The production of the mock-up at the end of the investigation cycle was actually logged in the Quality Log as the next review on Wednesday of the second week. The entry on the Quality Log referred to it as 'Delegate Handout Pack – Exploration Timebox – Iteration One'.

Sanjay had suggested that Chris need not use the Quality Log to track this and just turn up to the reviews. However, Chris had many other products to look after at the moment and wanted to be more formal on this occasion.

Various DSDM Atern techniques are being used during this timebox and particularly the use of modelling and iterative development. Visualisations and partial builds of the delegate handout pack and its sub-products increased the understanding of what the problems were and what the solutions may be. It also helped give Sanjay visibility of progress to see how the timebox was going.

Informal communication was helping, too. Everyone knew that putting sun cream into the bag was easy and they may do it anyway, but they can decide very late on. They were thinking of upgrading the pen to a laser pen, but they needed to check out what kind of batteries they ran on. None of this had been written down and if it was getting too tight on any deadline they would drop it.

Days 6–8

On Day 6 a problem was identified. Including the furry toy meant that the case would not close so they decided to drop this idea out and put in the drinks coaster instead.

On the morning of Day 8 Mary and Adrian were to finish off the presentations to go into the mock-up of the delegate handout pack, but another problem had arisen. The drinks coaster was made of glass and Linda was concerned that it was likely to break, which would be a safety hazard. The team had to decide what to do. Mary and Adrian did not have the time to investigate options with Linda – in fact they could do with some help from her.

So Sanjay said he would look into an alternative coaster, but for the time being the team would include the sun cream and the pencil for the review this afternoon. His decision was based on what the business would want and not what would be technically easy for the team. Linda then helped with the presentations.

Both of these problems had been spotted early as risks because they had been captured in the wash-up meetings which took place at the end of each day throughout the timebox. This allowed Sanjay to keep a close eye on things.

Day 9 – Consolidation

The team was very focused on getting the final deliverable agreed on Friday afternoon. Four sponsors happen to be in the office that day and they will be present at the final review – there will be no second chance. Next week the same team would be working on the publicity materials and press releases. They already had a room booked for a workshop on Monday afternoon – the delegate handout pack timebox could not overrun.

The consolidation review went well and for completeness the team decided to finish the original Product Description so that they could refer to it at a later date if it was needed for another conference. In effect they had defined it by creating it!

11.2 VARIATIONS

The scenario is a very simple one. They are many variations that could have taken place. Here are a few considerations that were left out for the sake of brevity.

11.2.1 Quality criteria

Even though team members were unsure about the best way to go, they could have still used a degree of quality criteria. Examples could be:

- Can I get 100 of them (whatever they are) to the venue easily? (Bags would probably be yes, but Bonsai trees perhaps no)
- Is everything in English?
- Can we put sponsorship on it?
- Can we have it near food?

11.2.2 Product Description

The Product Description could have been created earlier. The example shows a situation where the Product Description was written at the very end. Often in PRINCE2 the Product Description is written at the very beginning. Whether using agile project management or not, the decision needs to be made of when to write the Product Description. It is important to remember that the fundamental question here is knowing when a specialist product moves from requirement mode to solution mode.

It is often the case that a team will have very little idea of composition, derivation, format and presentation at an early stage.

11.2.3 Separate Solution Tester

It would be preferable to have a separate Solution Tester. Independent checking of the product is often better than using the Solution Developer. However, this is often dictated by team size.

11.2.4 Technical Coordinator and Business Visionary

The Technical Coordinator and Business Visionary are not mentioned in the example. They would be involved in the reviews and would be acting on behalf of the Project Board to check the technical design of the bag (would it work?) and its appropriateness in the wider business context (are we creating the right thing?).

11.2.5 Business Advisers

The role of the Business Adviser could have been expanded to include more people. Someone from Health and Safety could have been involved or even valued customers. This would help to create more validation and buy-in.

11.2.6 Combined pizzas

The example used a timebox which was for an exploration pizza. A subsequent timebox could be where the bag was physically made 'for real' and this would be an engineering timebox only.

There is always the option, and it is quite typical, to combine both phases into one timebox. In the example this could have been done by creating a three-week timebox where the first half was very much exploration and the second half was more to do with engineering. There is normally a point in the timebox where it is not obvious which pizza the team is in because they are in a transition from understanding the problem to delivering the solution.

11.2.7 The Prioritised Requirements List

The PRL in the example could not have been simpler. Although this may suffice occasionally, it would normally be a lot more detailed. Other columns could include estimates of time, cost or value, the last being particularly useful on agile projects.

11.2.8 Appropriateness of levels

This example focused on a single item at a low level of the overall Product Breakdown Structure, but the same concept applies to all levels and all plans. The same approach could have been used for the conference as a whole. One difference that can occur is that products already exist and had only to be selected. It may not be necessary to model or prototype the conference venue.

11.2.9 Timebox duration

As with the levels just mentioned, the same concept applies to a timebox of any duration. A timebox can be six months long. The most important factor is that the lowest level of timebox (called a development timebox in DSDM

Atern) should not be more than two to six weeks long in order to keep a project under control.

On higher-level timeboxes (called project or increment timeboxes) it may not be necessary to use the three cycles (IRC).

11.2.10 Technical stages

In effect the two pizzas and deployment represent the technical stages mentioned in PRINCE2. Iterative and incremental development of a product doesn't need to be done in a linear fashion using such terms as analysis, design, build, test and implement. All of these technical stages are being carried out, but it could be said they are all happening at once. As soon as the bag was being drawn on a flipchart it was being analysed, designed, built and tested. Perhaps the only stage not obvious is the fact that it is being built. DSDM Atern sees this as evolutionary building.

11.2.11 The principles

All eight of the principles were being used during the example with the exception perhaps of the incremental delivery part of Principle 6. However, although the bag was not delivered incrementally (it was built iteratively) it could represent an incremental delivery to the wider conference project as a whole.

11.2.12 Using Planning (PL) to create the timebox

On this particular example it may have been appropriate to use Planning (PL) to create the timebox plan, but it would have been a very light version, perhaps with sticky notes on a wall as opposed to activity networks and Gantt charts.

Product-based planning would have been used as far as it could be. There would be emerging Product Descriptions and quite often the Product Flow Diagram looks very much like a timebox plan anyway.

12 Conclusion

The preceding chapters have described how to bring PRINCE2 and DSDM Atern together to work as a combined method for project management and product delivery.

The text has explained what they are, what their strengths are and the merits of combining the two. It has given detailed guidance on how to adjust PRINCE2 in order to integrate with DSDM Atern by examining the process models, organisation structures, components and techniques of each approach.

The most important part of the publication has been to describe why the two methods should be combined and the benefits this brings. There is a saying 'If it ain't broke don't fix it.' When looking at current practices in project management today, the question to be addressed is whether or not these practices are good enough or if there is room for improvement.

In today's world a successful project is commonly regarded as a bonus rather than a matter of course and therefore even though current project management practices may not necessarily be 'broke', there could still be room for more evolution to take place.

Darwinism applies to project management methods and in past decades ideas have come and gone through natural selection, as the climate in which they operate has changed. In the 1980s change was a slow process and there wasn't a huge desire to move quickly. A bank was a place where people kept their money and a supermarket sold groceries. The resultant methods were therefore slow and thorough.

Things started to change in the 1990s when organisations needed to move quickly to stay ahead. In the IT sector this led to rapid application development (RAD), but it soon fell into disrepute and then into general disuse as the short-term speed came with a lack of rigour and technical vision.

This gave rise to the creation of DSDM Atern in the mid-1990s and with the widespread take up of PRINCE2 around the turn of the century there was now a new set of ideas to address the needs of a new digital world of the internet where banks can add credit to a mobile phone and supermarkets are banks!

Today's organisations in all sectors need their project management processes to be rigorous yet flexible. As methods evolve and are naturally selected the key question is one of balance. Just as too much rigour is detrimental, so is too little.

The text has described how and why integrating PRINCE2 with DSDM Atern can address this question of balance. In blending the two methods it gives thoroughness and flexibility through strong governance and dynamic product delivery. Both approaches are inherently scalable, tailorable and adaptable in order to create something which is fit for purpose for any project in any environment.

However, there is perhaps a bigger question to answer and it concerns the ability of any organisation to adopt this new combined approach. Can an organisation's culture adapt to this way of working?

Individuals may want to work in this way, but will the ethos and culture of an organisation support this or will it prevent it?

One of the most successful ways to introduce new tools, techniques and processes to any organisation is with the involvement of the people affected by it. Many of the reasons for integrating PRINCE2 with DSDM Atern support the view that the two methods give a natural way in which people want to work. These methods accept the need for rigour, but also allow informality when it is appropriate.

Integrating PRINCE2 with DSDM Atern relies on the acceptance that a good process is important, but the need to leverage the people using it is vital. It is this latter point which is the natural focus of integrating PRINCE2 with DSDM Atern. If people are empowered and collaborate from within a structure of good governance, the chances of success are greatly increased. However, if the people in an organisation feel exposed to a culture of blame, they will become defensive and the dynamism will not be there.

In the final analysis it is often a question of culture. If people want to work this way they can – and if they can't, they won't!

In summary, it seems appropriate to adapt the well-known saying of the car manufacturer Henry Ford:

'If an organisation thinks it can do a thing or thinks it can't do a thing, it's right.'

Part 4
Appendices

Appendix A: Guidance on tailoring the PRINCE2 management products

Table A.1 outlines suggested changes to the PRINCE2 management products. It does not mean that the full set has to be produced on every project. Although they are commonly thought of as documents they are in fact sets of information. An example of this is that an Exception Report could be a phone call and not a document.

Table A.1 Suggested changes to the PRINCE2 management products

Ref. no.	Management product	Guidance
A1	Acceptance Criteria	It may be appropriate to MoSCoW 'Major Functions'.
A2	Business Case	It may be appropriate to mention the use of the agile approach (under 'Options') if this directly affects the viability of the project. 'Benefits Expected' would need to be qualified by the assumption of how much is likely to be delivered.
A3	Checkpoint Report	If a Work Package contains a timebox then information on its status will need to be included into the existing composition. A new heading 'Timebox Status' is needed. This could replace the need for 'Work Package Tolerance Status' in most cases.
A4	Communication Plan	No specific changes needed to the composition, but it would be important to state where teams will be using informal lines of communication to relay certain types of information e.g. daily wash-ups.
A5	Configuration Item Record (CIR)	No specific changes needed to the composition, but it should be realised that Configuration Management can be more volatile when integrating PRINCE2 with DSDM Atern and therefore CIRs (and the related Product Descriptions) need to be at the appropriate level to support this.
A6	Configuration Management Plan	Needs an additional heading ('DSDM Atern Considerations') to record the extra guidance needed to cater for the specific needs of controlling products undergoing iterative development and incremental delivery. It needs to be made clear how much responsibility for Configuration Management lies within the product delivery team.
A7	Customer's quality expectations	No change.
A8	Daily Log	No changes to the composition are required. This product could be used to record any headlines from the daily wash-ups or act as a project diary.
A9	End Project Report	The following extra heading should be added: 'Performance against Scope', explaining how much of the scope was delivered (as derived from the PRL). Ideally this would be expressed in measurable terms such as 'Value Delivered'.

Table A.1 Suggested changes to the PRINCE2 management products ... continued

Ref. no.	Management product	Guidance
A10	End Stage Report	The following extra heading should be added: 'Performance against Scope' explaining how much of the scope was delivered (as derived from the PRL). Ideally this would be expressed in measurable terms such as 'Value Delivered'.
A11	Exception Plan	No change to the composition. This may also be referred to as an exception timebox.
A12	Exception Report	No change to the composition of this product is necessary, but it would be appropriate to mention 'Scope' specifically when describing the consequences of any deviation and assessing the available options.
A13	Follow-on Action Recommendations	Could prove useful to add a suggested MoSCoW value to each Request for Change or Off-Specification.
A14	Highlight Report	Needs an additional heading 'Scope Status', which would contain information about how many features have been dropped or added in and how important they are.
A15	Issue Log	No change needed although priority could be populated using MoSCoW.
A16	Lessons Learned Log	No change to the composition of this product is necessary, but it could be appropriate to separate out the heading 'Project Management Method' to capture specifics about running PRINCE2 with DSDM Atern.
A17	Lessons Learned Report	Needs an additional heading 'Process Evaluation' outlining feedback about how the PRINCE2 process worked with DSDM Atern.
A18	Off-Specification	No change.
A19	Post-project Review Plan	No change to this specific product, but an additional product is required to assess the value of any incremental delivery which has taken place. The DSDM Atern Project Review Report can be used as a holding area for this.
A20	Product Breakdown Structure	No change. (See Chapter 10 for specific guidance when using PRINCE2 with DSDM Atern.)
A21	Product Checklist	No change. A decision would need to be taken during Setting up Project Controls (IP4) to decide whether or not to include iterations of individual products. This would need to link in with the approach to timeboxing and Work Packages as discussed in Chapter 10.
A22	Product Description	No change to the composition of this product. The level of detail and the baselining of the description of a specialist product are discussed in Chapter 9.
A23	Product Flow Diagram	No change. (See Chapter 10 for specific guidance when using PRINCE2 with DSDM Atern.)

Table A.1 Suggested changes to the PRINCE2 management products ... continued

Ref. no.	Management product	Guidance
A24	Product Status Account	It may be appropriate to add 'Iteration Information' to the list of headings included under 'Additional Information'.
A25	Project Approach	Although there is not a specific requirement for this product to mention the project management approach, it is advisable to note that PRINCE2 is running with DSDM Atern so that the Project Board can be made aware of it. A project integrating PRINCE2 with DSDM Atern will exhibit many different characteristics from a PRINCE2-only project and this will affect concepts such as management by exception.
A26	Project Brief	When compiling this product 'Project Scope' should be promoted to a first-level heading and entries should be MoSCoWed. It is possible at this early point in the overall process that most (if not all) of the entries are prioritised as 'Musts'. This is normal because they will be describing generic high-level features.
A27	Project Initiation Document (PID)	The PID comprises a collection of PRINCE2 management products and therefore any changes to them are mentioned elsewhere in Appendix A. The PID will need to include the additional DSDM Atern products and this is covered in detail in Chapter 7.
A28	Project Issue	No change needed although priority could be populated using MoSCoW.
A29	Project Mandate	It may be appropriate to add the extra heading 'Suggested Project Management Approach'. This would enable corporate or programme management to recommend a particular approach for the project (e.g. running PRINCE2 with DSDM Atern).
A30	Project Plan	No change to the composition, but it is recommended to document how the scope is to be managed with respect to tolerances and contingency plans under the relevant headings or under 'planning assumptions'.
A31	Project Quality Plan	No change to the composition, but the quality techniques and standards used on a project integrating PRINCE2 with DSDM Atern may be significantly different from other PRINCE2-only projects (see Chapter 9 for guidance). The integration of PRINCE2 and DSDM Atern could be described here.
A32	Quality Log	This product can be left with its existing composition or adjusted to provide more information on iteration and timeboxes. If iteration information is to be added this would require a new heading of 'Iteration' or 'Iteration Type'. However, this may prove too detailed for a Project Manager at Assessing Progress (CS2). Also early iterations (e.g. Investigate and Refine) may not be regarded as a 'Pass' or a 'Fail'. If timebox information is to be added this would require the new heading 'Timebox Reference', with information about which timebox produced it. An additional field of 'Timebox Owner' could also be added if desired.
A33	Request for Change	No change.

Table A.1 Suggested changes to the PRINCE2 management products ... continued

Ref. no.	Management product	Guidance
A34	Risk Log	No change.
A35	Stage Plan	'Plan Description' would include brief guidance on the use of increments if appropriate (under 'Planned Approach'). May need an additional sub-heading 'Timebox Control' beneath 'Quality Plan'. This would contain techniques and standards to be used to ensure that Work Package timeboxes have been executed and completed correctly. However, it would not be necessary to show quality control methods, timings and resources on the Stage Quality Plan if this is handled from within the Work Package timebox.
A36	Work Package	If a Work Package contains a timebox then the following changes are needed: 'Joint Agreement on Effort, Cost, Start and End Dates, and Tolerances' should be replaced by 'Timebox Details', which would describe who is in the timebox team and the start and end dates. The Team Manager would lead the timebox. 'Work Package Description' would need to use the word 'Timebox' with an appropriate name and description. Throughout the completion of each entry in the Work Package composition it would be necessary to state clearly what activities will be handled within the timebox, e.g. 'Configuration Management requirements' could be done at Project Manager level when Receiving Completed Work Package (CS9) or alternatively could be handled from within the timebox during Executing a Work Package (MP2).

Appendix B: Terminology used in DSDM v4.2

Table B.1 The nine principles of DSDM v4.2

Principle	Incorporated into
Active user involvement is imperative	■ Collaborate
DSDM teams must be empowered to make decisions	■ Collaborate
The focus is on frequent delivery of products	■ Demonstrate control
Fitness for business purpose is the essential criterion for acceptance of deliverables	■ Focus on the business need
Iterative and incremental development is necessary to converge on an accurate business solution	■ Develop iteratively ■ Build incrementally from firm foundations
All changes during development are reversible	■ Develop iteratively
Requirements are baselined at a high level	■ Build incrementally from firm foundations
Testing is integrated throughout the lifecycle	■ Never compromise quality
A collaborative and cooperative approach between all stakeholders is essential	■ Collaborate

Table B.2 The lifecycle phases of DSDM v4.2

Lifecycle phase	New name
Pre-project	Pre-project
Feasibility study	Feasibility
Business study	Foundations
Functional model iteration	Exploration
Design and build iteration	Engineering
Implementation	Deployment
Post-project	Post-project

Table B.3 The roles in DSDM v4.2

Role:	New name:
Executive Sponsor	Business Sponsor
Visionary	Business Visionary
Ambassador User	Business Ambassador
Adviser User	Business Adviser
Project Manager	Project Manager
Team Leader	Team Leader
Technical Coordinator	Technical Coordinator
Developer	Solution Developer
Tester	Solution Tester

Appendix C: Further information

For more information on training in DSDM Atern, case studies, white papers and membership of the DSDM Consortium please visit www.dsdm.org

If you are new to DSDM Atern you may want to consider the Foundation Exam. This level aims to measure whether a candidate would be able to act as an informed member of a Project Management Team using DSDM within a project environment supporting DSDM. To this end candidates need to show they understand the principles and terminology of the framework. Visit www.apmgroup.co.uk for more information.

PRINCE2 PUBLICATIONS

OGC (2002) *People Issues and PRINCE2™*. The Stationery Office, London. ISBN-10: 0113308965; ISBN-13: 978-0113308965.

OGC (2002) *Tailoring PRINCE2*. The Stationery Office, London. ISBN-10: 0113308973; ISBN-13: 978-0113308972.

OGC (2005) *Managing Successful Projects with PRINCE2*. The Stationery Office, London. ISBN-10: 0113309465; ISBN-13: 978-0113309467.

OGC (2006) *Business Benefits through Programme and Project Management*. The Stationery Office, London. ISBN-10: 0113310250; ISBN-13: 978-0113310258.

OGC (2006) *PRINCE2 for the Project Executive: Practical Advice for Achieving Project Governance*. The Stationery Office, London. ISBN-10: 0113309678; ISBN-13: 978-0113309672.

OGC (2007) *Improving Project Performance using P2MM*. The Stationery Office, London. ISBN-10: 0113310315; ISBN-13: 978-0113310319.

Publications are available in a variety of formats and can be purchased from www.best-management-practice.com

USEFUL LINKS

www.best-management-practice.com – the OGC official umbrella site, dedicated to making access to best management practice guidance quick and easy, and providing support for all levels of adoption of the OGC Best Practice guidance.

www.usergroup.org.uk – the official PRINCE2™ user group.

www.apmg-icp.com – Agile Special Interest Group.

PRINCE2 ACCREDITATION

There are two levels of qualification:

- Foundation – This level aims to measure whether a candidate would be able to act as an informed member of a Project Management Team on a project using the PRINCE2™ method, within an environment supporting PRINCE2™. To this end candidates need to show they understand the principles and terminology of the method.
- Practitioner – This level aims to measure whether a candidate would be able to apply PRINCE2™ to the running and managing of a project within an environment supporting PRINCE2™. To this end they need to exhibit the competence required for the foundation qualification, and show that they can apply and tune PRINCE2™ to address the needs and problems of a specific project scenario.

For more information on accredited training organisations and the exams please visit www.prince2.org.uk

Appendix D: Glossaries

DSDM GLOSSARY

80:20 rule
A rule of thumb stating that 80% of consequences stem from 20% of causes. Also known as the Pareto Principle, it advocates pragmatism on a DSDM Atern project.

BAD
The business area definition. An element of the business foundations product produced during the foundations phase.

Cheese
A colloquialism for the feasibility and foundations phases, which are represented on the DSDM Atern lifecycle diagram as a cheese-wedge shape.

Deployment
A phase that focuses on getting the solution or part of it into operational use.

Element
A part of a product from the DSDM Atern lifecycle. It may be a paragraph or a document in its own right.

Engineering
A phase that is used iteratively and incrementally to evolve the solution created during exploration.

Exploration
A phase that is used iteratively and incrementally to investigate the detailed requirements and translate them into a form which can then be evolved into a viable solution.

Feasibility
A phase that gives the first opportunity for deciding whether or not the project is viable from a technical or business perspective.

Foundations
A phase to establish firm and enduring foundations from the three perspectives on a project of business, solution and management.

Function/Feature
See Requirement.

Increment
1. A partial delivery of the final product, preferably into operational use if possible

2. A part of the project which creates the partial delivery.

Iteration
1. A general term for working in a cyclic way where several attempts are made in order to get a more accurate or beneficial result

2. One cycle of Identify, Plan, Evolve and Review, which takes place inside a timebox.

MoSCoW
A prioritisation technique mainly used on Requirements, where M stands for Must Haves, S stands for Should Haves, C stands for Could Haves and W stands for Won't Haves this time around.

Pizza
A colloquialism for either the exploration phase or the engineering phase of a project, which are shown as round circles on the DSDM Atern lifecycle diagram.

Post-Project
Takes place after the last planned deployment. It is used to assess the business value delivered by the project.

Pre-project
A phase where the initial idea or imperative is formalised in order to initiate a project.

Principle

A 'natural law', which acts as an attitude to take and a mindset to adopt on a DSDM Atern project.

Requirement

Something the final product needs to be able to do or to do to a certain level of performance. Similar to 'function' and 'feature'.

ROI

Return on investment.

Solution architecture definition (SAD)

An element of the solution foundations product produced during the foundations phase.

Scope

A description of what the product will do and what it will not do. This could be a list of features and/or a description of areas of the business which may or may not be affected.

Prioritised Requirements List (PRL)

A document holding a list of requirements for the final product which have been prioritised using the MoSCoW technique. It may also hold other information such as estimates and actuals.

Timebox

A period of time, at the end of which an objective has been met. The objective would typically be a deliverable of some sort. There are different types of timebox operating at different levels. They are project, increment and development. A timebox is managed by adding or removing content in order to meet the timebox objective.

UTH rule

A rule that requirements will grow in number as each DSDM Atern phase is passed through. The letters stand for units, tens and hundreds.

PRINCE2 GLOSSARY

Acceptance Criteria
A prioritised list of criteria that the final product(s) must meet before the customer will accept them.

Activity Network
A flow diagram showing the activities of a plan and their interdependencies. The network shows each activity's duration, earliest start and finish times, latest start and finish times and float. Also known as 'planning network'.

Baseline
Reference levels against which an entity is monitored and controlled.

Benefits
The quantifiable and measurable improvement resulting from an outcome which is perceived as positive by a stakeholder and which will normally have a tangible value expressed in monetary or resource terms. Benefits are expected when a change is conceived. Benefits are realised as a result of activities undertaken to effect the change.

Business Case
The justification for an initiative (programme, project, activity), which typically contains costs, benefits, risks and timescales and against which continuing viability is tested.

Change Control
The procedure to ensure that the processing of all Project Issues is controlled, including submission, analysis and decision-making.

Checkpoint Report
A progress report of the information gathered at a checkpoint meeting which is given by a team to the Project Manager and provides reporting data as defined in the Work Package.

Communication Plan
A plan of the communications activities during the organisational activity (strategic, programme, project or operational). It typically contains when, what, how and with whom information flows will be established and maintained.

Configuration Management
The discipline that gives management appropriate control over relevant assets. Typically includes planning, identification, control, reporting and reviewing.

Customer
The person or group who commissioned the work and will benefit from the end results.

Customer's quality expectations (CQE)
A statement from the customer about the quality expected from the final product.

Daily Log
A record of jobs to do or to check that others have done, commitments from the author or others, important events, decisions or discussions.

Deliverables
An item that the project has to create as part of the requirements. It may be part of the final outcome or an intermediate element on which one or more subsequent deliverables are dependent. According to the type of project, another name for a deliverable is 'product'.

Earned value analysis
Earned value analysis is a method for measuring project performance. It indicates how much of the budget should have been spent in view of the amount of work done so far and the task, assignment or resources.

End Project Report

A report given by the Project Manager to the Project Board that confirms the handover of all products and provides an updated Business Case and an assessment of how well the project has done against its Project Initiation Document.

End Stage Report

A report given by the Project Manager to the Project Board at the end of each management stage of the project. It provides information about the project performance during the stage and the project status at stage end.

Exception Assessment

A meeting of the Project Board to approve (or reject) an Exception Plan.

Exception Plan

A plan that often follows an Exception Report. For a Team Plan exception, it covers the period from the present to the end of the Work Package; for a Stage Plan exception, it covers the period from the present to the end of the current stage. If the exception were at a project level, the Project Plan would be replaced.

Exception Report

Description of the exception situation, its impact, options, recommendation and impact of the recommendation to the Project Board.

Executive

The single individual with overall responsibility for ensuring that a project meets its objectives and delivers the projected benefits. This individual should ensure that the project or programme maintains its business focus, that it has clear authority and that the work, including risks, is actively managed. The Executive is the chairperson of the Project Board, representing the customer, and is the owner of the Business Case.

Feasibility study

A feasibility study is an early study of a problem to assess if a solution is feasible. The study will normally scope the problem, identify and explore a number of solutions, and make a recommendation on what action to take. Part of the work in developing options is to calculate an outline Business Case for each as one aspect of comparison.

Gantt chart

This is a diagram of a plan's activities against a time background, showing start and end times and resources required.

Highlight Report

Time-driven report from the Project Manager to the Project Board on stage progress.

Issue Log

Contains all Project Issues including requests for change raised during the project.

Lessons Learned Log

An informal collection of good and bad lessons learned about the management and specialist processes and products as the project progresses.

Lessons Learned Report

A report that describes the lessons learned in undertaking the project and includes statistics from the quality control of the project's management products. It is approved by the Project Board and then held centrally for the benefit of future projects.

Off-Specification

Something that should be provided by the project, but currently is not (or is forecast not to be) provided.

Operational and maintenance acceptance

Acceptance by the person or group who will support the product during its useful life that it is accepted into the operational environment. The format of the acceptance will depend on the product itself – it could be in the form of an acceptance letter signed by the appropriate authority, or a more complex report detailing the operational and maintenance arrangements that have been put in place.

Outcome

The result of change, normally affecting real-world behaviour and/or circumstances. Outcomes are desired when a change is conceived. Outcomes are achieved as a result of the activities undertaken to effect the change.

Output

The tangible or intangible artefact produced, constructed or created as a result of a planned activity.

Phase

A part, section or segment of a project, similar in meaning to a PRINCE2 stage. The key meaning of stage in PRINCE2 terms is the use of management stages – sections of the project to which the Project Board commits one at a time. A phase might be more connected to a time slice, change of skills required or change of emphasis.

PRINCE2

A method that supports some selected aspects of project management. The acronym stands for PRojects IN Controlled Environments.

Process

That which must be done to bring about a particular result in terms of information to be gathered, decisions to be made and results to be achieved.

Product

An input or output, whether tangible or intangible, that can be described in advance, created and tested. Also known as an output or deliverable.

Product-based planning

A four-step technique leading to a comprehensive plan based on creation and delivery of required outputs. The technique considers prerequisite products, quality requirements and the dependencies between products.

Product Breakdown Structure (PBS)

A hierarchy of all the products to be produced during a plan.

Product Checklist

A list of the major products of a plan, plus key dates in their delivery.

Product Description (PD)

A description of a product's purpose, composition, derivation and quality criteria. It is produced at planning time, as soon as possible after the need for the product is identified.

Product Flow Diagram (PFD)

A diagram showing the sequence of production and interdependencies of the products listed in a Product Breakdown Structure.

Product Status Account

A report on the status of products. The required products can be specified by identifier or the part of the project in which they were developed.

Programme

A set of projects and activities that are coordinated and managed as a unit such that they achieve outcomes and realise benefits.

Project

A temporary organisation that is created for the purpose of delivering one or more business products according to a specified Business Case.

Project Approach

A description of the way in which the work of the project is to be approached. It might be created after answering the questions: Are we building a product from scratch or buying in a product that already exists? Are the technology and products that we can use constrained by decisions taken at programme level?

Project Assurance

The Project Board's responsibilities to assure itself that the project is being conducted correctly.

Project Brief

Statement that describes the purpose, cost, time and performance requirements and constraints for a project.

Project Initiation Document (PID)

A logical document that brings together the key information needed to start the project on a sound basis and to convey that information to all concerned with the project.

Project Issue

A term used to cover any concern, query, Request for Change, suggestion or Off-Specification raised during the project.

Project management

The planning, monitoring and control of all aspects of a project and the motivation of all those involved in it to achieve the project objectives on time and to the specified cost, quality and performance.

Project Management Team

Covers the entire management structure of Project Board, Project Manager, plus any Team Manager, Project Assurance and Project Support roles.

Project Manager

The person given the authority and responsibility to manage the project on a day-to-day basis to deliver the required products within the constraints agreed with the Project Board.

Project Mandate

Information created externally to the project that forms the terms of reference and is used to start up the PRINCE2 project.

Project Plan

A high-level plan showing the major products of the project, when they will be delivered and at what cost.

Project Quality Plan

A plan defining the key quality criteria, quality control and audit processes to be applied to project management and specialist work in the PRINCE2 project.

Project Support

An administrative role in the Project Management Team. Project Support can be in the form of advice and help with project management tools, guidance, administrative services such as filing, and the collection of actual data.

Quality

The totality of features and characteristics of a product or service that bear on its ability to satisfy stated needs. Also defined as 'fitness for purpose' or 'conforms to requirements'.

Quality Log

Contains all planned and completed quality activities.

Quality review

A quality review is a quality checking technique with a specific structure, defined roles and procedure designed to ensure a product's completeness and adherence to standards. The participants are drawn from those with an interest in the product and those with the necessary skills to review its correctness. An example of the checks made by a quality review is finding out whether the document matches the quality criteria in the Product Description.

Request for Change (RFC)

A means of proposing a modification to the current specification of a product. It is one type of Project Issue.

Requirements

A description of the user's needs. See also Specification.

Reviewer

A person asked to review a product that is the subject of a quality review.

Risk

An uncertain event or set of events which, should it occur, will have an effect on the achievement of objectives. A risk is measured by a combination of the probability of a perceived threat or opportunity occurring and the magnitude of its impact on objectives.

Risk Log

A record of all identified risks relating to an initiative with their status and history. Also called a Risk Register.

Senior Supplier (SS)

The Project Board role that provides knowledge and experience of the main discipline(s) involved in the production of the project's deliverable(s). Represents the supplier interests within the project and provides supplier resources.

Senior User (SU)

The Project Board role accountable for ensuring that user needs are specified correctly and that the solution meets those needs.

Specification

A detailed statement of what the user wants in terms of products, what these should look like, what they should do and with what they should interface.

Sponsor

The main driving force behind a programme or project.

Stage

A stage is the section of the project that the Project Manager is managing on behalf of the Project Board at any one time, at the end of which the Project Board wishes to review progress to date, the state of the Project Plan, Business Case and risks, and the next Stage Plan in order to decide whether to continue with the project.

Stakeholders

Any individual, group or organisation that can affect, be affected by, or perceive itself to be affected by, an initiative (programme, project, activity, risk).

Supplier

The group or groups responsible for the supply of the project's specialist products.

Team Manager

A role that may be employed by the Project Manager or Senior Supplier to manage the work of project team members.

Tolerance

The permissible deviation above and below a plan's estimate of time and cost without escalating the deviation to the next level of management.

User(s)

The person or group who will use the final deliverable(s) of the project.

Work Package

The set of information relevant to the creation of one or more products.

Index

Index

Acceptance Criteria 73
Agile Alliance 3
agility 24–5
Atern see DSDM Atern
authorising a timebox 38–9
Authorising Work Package (CS1) 38–9

BAD (Business Area Definition) 38
baselining 27
    Product Descriptions 47, 57
Business Adviser 44, 66
Business Ambassador 22, 44
Business Analyst 22, 45
Business Area Definition (BAD) 38
Business Case 12, 14, 46, 73
business involvement 22
business needs 16
Business Sponsor 45
Business Visionary 44, 66

ceremony assessment 16
change 26–7, 50
Change Control 14, 28, 51–2
Checkpoint Report 73
Closing a Project (CP) 41
collaboration 17
communication 18
    informal 20, 47–8
    rich 20
Communication Plan 48, 73
Configuration Item Record (CIR) 73
Configuration Management 14, 51
    iterative development 51
Configuration Management Plan 73
control over projects 18
controlled close 49

controlled progress 48–9
controlled start, mapping 36–7, 37–8
Controlling a Stage (CS) 40
controls 47–9
CP (Closing a Project) 41
CS1 (Authorising Work Package) 38–9
CS (Controlling a Stage) 40
Customer's quality expectations 73

Daily Log 73
delivery 24, 25, 28–9, 42
delivery on time 16–17
Directing a Project (DP) 41
documentation 6–7, 26
DP (Directing a Project) 41
DSDM see Dynamic Systems Development Method
DSDM Atern 3, 4
    advantages of using 16–23
    Business Adviser 44
    Business Ambassador 22, 44
    Business Analyst 45
    Business Sponsor 45
    Business Visionary 44
    Coach 45
    components 11
    controls 49
    delivery 24, 25
    facilitated workshops 55
    iterative development 55–6
    lifecycle 33–5
    modelling 56
    MoSCoW prioritisation 56
    overview 10–11
    PRINCE2
        combined organisational structure 42–5
        combined process model 33–41

differences from 24–5
integration with 24–9
mapping 36–7, 37–8
similarities to 24
principles 16–18, 67
Project Approach Questionnaire 49
Project Manager 45
prototyping 55–6
risk management 49–50
roles 44–5
scenario 61–9
Solution Developer 45
Solution Tester 45
Team Leader 44
Technical Coordinator 44
timeboxing 53–5
wash ups 49–50
Dynamic Systems Development Method (DSDM) 3–4, 10
terminology 77
versions 7

End Project Report 73
End Stage Assessment 49
End Stage Report 74
estimates 20
Exception Assessment 49
Exception Plan 47, 74
Exception Report 48, 74
external risks 50

facilitated workshops 20, 22, 55
features of projects 18
flexing requirements 18–19
Follow-on Action Recommendations 74

governance roles 42

Highlight Report 48, 74
horizontal product development 39

incremental development 17, 22–3, 38–9
Initiating a Project (IP) 40
iron triangle 13
Issue Log 74
iterative development 17, 20, 22, 26, 38–9, 55–6
Configuration Management 51

Lessons Learned Log 74
lifecycles see process models

management by exception 9, 12, 48
management stages 12–13, 48
Managing Product Delivery (MP) 38, 40
Managing Stage Boundaries (SB) 40
method, definition 7
method spectrum 4, 5
modelling 20, 56
MoSCoW prioritisation 20–21, 56, 57
MP (Managing Product Delivery) 38, 40

Off-Specification 74
organisational structure for PRINCE2 46–7

PAQ (Project Approach Questionnaire) 49
PID see Product Initiation Document
PID lite 38
PL (Planning) 41, 67
planning, product-based 13
Planning (PL) 41, 67
plans 47
Post-project Review Plan 74
PRINCE2 3–4
Acceptance Criteria 73
advantages of using 12–15
agility 24–5
Business Case 46, 73
Checkpoint Report 73
Closing a Project (CP) 41

Communication Plan 73
components 9
Configuration Item Record (CIR) 73
Configuration Management Plan 73
Controlling a Stage (CS) 40
controls 47
customer's quality expectations 73
Daily Log 73
Directing a Project (DP) 41
DSDM Atern
    combined organisational structure 42–5
    combined process model 33–41
    differences from 24–5
    integration with 24–9
    mapping 36–7, 37–8
    similarities to 24
End Project Report 73
End Stage Report 74
Exception Plan 74
Exception Report 74
Follow-on Action Recommendations 74
Highlight Report 74
Initiating a Project (IP) 40
Issue Log 74
Lessons Learned Log 74
Managing Product Delivery (MP) 40
Managing Stage Boundaries (SB) 40
Off-Specification 74
organisational structure 46–7
overview 8–9
Planning (PL) 41
plans 47
Post-project Review Plan 74
process model 33–5
processes 9, 39–41
product-based planning 57
Product Breakdown Structure 74
Product Descriptions 74
Product Flow Diagram 74

Product Status Account 75
Project Approach 75
Project Board 42
Project Brief 75
Project Initiation Document (PID) 75
Project Issues 75
Project Management Team 42–4
Project Manager 42
Project Mandate 75
Project Plan 75
Project Quality Plan 75
Project Support 44
Quality Log 75
Quality Review Technique 57–8
Request for Change 75
Risk Log 76
scenario 61–9
Stage Plan 76
Starting up a Project (SU) 40, 48
team manager 42
technical stages 67
versions 7
Work Packages 76
prioritisation 20–21, 56
Prioritised Requirements List (PRL) 21, 28, 38, 56, 57, 64, 66
process models 33–5
product-based planning 13, 57
Product Breakdown Structure 74
Product Descriptions 14, 24, 66, 74
    baselining 47, 57
Product Flow Diagram 74
Product Status Account 75
Project Approach 14, 75
Project Approach Questionnaire (PAQ) 38, 49
Project Assurance 14, 28, 50
Project Board 12, 42
    controls 48
Project Brief 14, 38, 75

Project Initiation Document (PID) 14, 36, 37, 48, 75
Project Issues 52, 75
project management
    agile 25
    convergent 4
    emergent 4
    by exception 9
    methods 4
    predictive 4
    principles 8
Project Management Team 42
Project Manager 42, 45
Project Mandate 14, 75
Project Plan 14, 75
Project Quality Plan 75
Project Support 44
projects
    parts of 12
    scope 52
prototyping 20, 22, 55–6

quality 17, 50–51
Quality Assurance 50
quality criteria 65–6
Quality Log 75
Quality Path 14
Quality Review Technique 14, 57–8

Request for Change 75
requirements 18
    definition 18–19
    planning 54
    prioritised list 21, 28, 35, 56, 57, 64, 66
rich communication 20
Risk Log 14, 76
risk management 49–50
risks, external 50

SAD (Solution Architecture Definition) 38

SB (Managing Stage Boundaries) 40
scope management 27–8
scope of project 52
Senior Supplier 28
Senior User 28
Solution Architecture Definition (SAD) 38
Solution Developer 45, 66
Solution Tester 45, 66
Stage Plan 76
Starting up a Project (SU) 40, 48

TCQ (time, cost and quality) triangle 13
Team Leader 44
team manager 42
Team Plan 39, 47
team structures 28
Technical Coordinator 44, 66
technical stages 67
Timebox Plan 39, 47
timeboxes 21–2, 24, 53–5
    combined 66
    content 53–4
    duration 66–7
    incremental 47
    levels 53
    Planning (PL) 67
tolerances 13, 48, 54–5

UTH (units, tens and hundreds) rule 18–19, 27, 28

vertical product development 39

wash ups 49–50
Work Packages 14, 34–5, 38–9, 76
    types 39
workshops, facilitated 20, 22